THOUGHTS OF GANDHI AND VINOBA

Gandhian Studies and Peace Research Series

1. Gandhian Model of Development and World Peace
   R.P. Misra (ed.)
2. Conflict Resolution through Non-Violence: Role of the Universities. Vol. 1: Science and Ethics
   K.D. Gangrade and **R.P. Misra** (eds.)
3. Conflict Resolution through Non-Violence: Role of the Universities, Vol. 2: Development without Destruction
   K.D. Gangrade and **R.P. Misra** (eds.)
4. The Social Philosophy of Mahatma Gandhi
   K.S. Bharathi
5. Gandhian Humanism
   Mohit Chakrabarti
6. Gandhian Holistic Economics
   Shashi Prabha Sharma
7. Gandhian Spiritualism: A Quest for the Essence of Excellence
   Mohit Chakrabarti
8. Gandhian Perspective on Population and Development
   A.K. Sharma
9. Thoughts of Gandhi and Vinoba
   K.S. Bharathi
10. Economic Philosophy of Mahatma Gandhi
    Shanti Swarup Gupta

About the Author

Dr. K.S. Bharathi did his Master's Degree in Gandhian Thought, Peace-Science, Economics, Political Science and History. He also did Postgraduate Diploma in Politics, Public Administration, Population Dynamics, Gandhian Thought, Tourism, Telgu and Business Management. He has contributed some articles in learned Journals in India and abroad. He is the author of : *Foundations of Gandhian Thought, Gandhi and Humanity, Socio-Religious Thoughts of Mahatma Gandhi, Gandhi and Ideology of Satyagraha, The Philosophy of Sarvodaya, Satyagraha of Mahatma Gandhi, Gandhi and Nehru, The Social Philosophy of Mahatma Gandhi, Foundations of Ambedkar Thought, Gandhian Approach to Rural Development, and Relevance of Gandhi.* At present, he is a faculty member in Postgraduate Department of Gandhian Thought of Nagpur University. He is the Chairman of the Board of Studies of Gandhian Thought, member of the Academic Council, member of the Faculty of Social Science and member of the Doctoral Research Committee of Nagpur University.

Gandhian Studies and Peace Research Series—9

THOUGHTS OF GANDHI AND VINOBA

K.S. BHARATHI
P.G. Department of Gandhian Thought
Nagpur University, Nagpur

CONCEPT PUBLISHING COMPANY, NEW DELHI 110059

ISBN 81-7022-543-4

First Published 1995

K.S. Bharathi (*b.* 1956)

Published and Printed by
Ashok Kumar Mittal
Concept Publishing Company
A/15-16, Commercial Block, Mohan Garden,
NEW DELHI 110059 (India)

DEDICATED
TO
J.C. KUMARAPPA

PREFACE

Gandhi and Vinoba looked upon spiritual life as the highest life and God realisation and self-realisation in this very life as the greatest achievement. Gandhi plunged into active service of the poorest as the means to that end. Vinoba renounced life along the path of Shankara.

Vinoba himself said that it was entirely due to Gandhi that he was led into the field of national activities. He has acknowledged very frankly his debt to Gandhi for initiation into selfless service of humanity. He acknowledged Gandhi as his Master in many matters but he was never a mere imitator.

Gandhi complimented Vinoba by calling him the First Satyagrahi. Vinoba has shown great originality in interpreting Gandhi's ideas and adding some new ideas of his own. After the death of Gandhi, Vinoba walked the whole length and breadth of the country spreading the message of Truth, Love and Compassion.

The life and work of Gandhi and Vinoba has been discussed in the first chapter. Philosophical thought of Gandhi and Vinoba has been covered in the second chapter. Ethical, Social, Economic and Political thoughts of Gandhi and Vinoba have been analysed in the next four chapters. Educational thought of Gandhi and Vinoba has been discussed in the last chapter.

I would like to place on record my indebtedness to scholars and thinkers whose ideas enabled me to bring out this book. I gratefully acknowledge the scholars from whose works I have drawn citations viz. Dr. K. Arunachalam, Dr. Vishwanath Tandon, Dr. R.R. Diwakar, Prof. Thakur Das Bang, Dr. Devendra Kumar, Dr. Usha Mehta, Gandhiji and Vinobaji.

So far as the writing of this book is concerned, whatever success I have achieved is due to the relentless efforts and encouragment of Dr. P.S.G. Kumar, Head, Department of Library and Information Science, Nagpur University. I sincerely express my gratitude to him.

I will be failing in my duty if I do not thank Mr. P.N. Hardas, P.G. Department of Gandhian Thought, Nagpur University, for his generous help in my endeavour.

I am indebted to Mr. Ashok Kumar Mittal of Concept Publishing Company for publishing this book in such a short span of time. Finally I hold myself to blame for the errors and shortcomings if any. This work would not have been completed without the grace of Lord Venkateswara of Tirumala and Alamelu Thayar of Tiruchanur.

K.S. BHARATHI

CONTENTS

1

LIFE AND WORK OF GANDHI AND VINOBA

Gandhiji was a great man. By any reckoning, he is one of the few outstanding personalities of the world in this century. Between the middle of the nineteenth and that of the twentieth centuries the world has seen a galaxy of great men who influenced their age in different ways. But none of them made greater impact on the thinking and actions of men than Gandhiji. His ideas and deeds permeated the entire human community. He was essentially a man who would be counted in the ages to come with the Buddha and Christ. He was the greatest of the humanists that India presented to the world in modern times.

Gandhiji was not a philosopher in the academic sense of the term. His ideas cannot be classed with any of the well-known schools of Indian philosophy. He was a practical man. In advocating his philosophy of action, he always advised men to take into account the psychological fact of human nature. He had tremendous faith in the goodness of man.

Mohandas Karamchand Gandhi was born on October 2, 1869, at Porbander in a middle class family of 'Vaishya Caste'. Porbander, one of the Kathiawad districts, is a coastal city on the west of Gujarat. The teachings of Buddha and Mahavira are much prevalent in his area. Karamchand Gandhi, known as Kaba Gandhi, married four times as he lost his first three wives in quick succession. His last wife, Putlibai, gave birth to a daughter and three sons. The youngest son was Mohandas. Karamchand Gandhi was the Dewan of Porbander. He was truthful, brave, honest and a man of principles. He never had any ambition to accumulate wealth and bequeathed his family very little property.

Gandhiji's mother, Putlibai, stood for religious faith and devotion. She had strict attitudes to alcohol and tobacco. Daily prayers and precise fasts were her routine. She had deep faith in religion and never took her food without daily prayers. Gandhiji inherited such qualities from her whose life was also founded on long struggles and experiments with truth. To quote Pyarelal, "He (Gandhi) revered his father, but his mother he adores... his father to him was the embodiment of uprightness, his mother of piety.... His mother became the core of his inner being. Her affection of forged bonds that continued to protect and influence him even when physically she was away and even ceased to be".[1] The family atmosphere of Gandhiji was religious.

Gandhiji had his primary and high school education at Rajkot. He was regular and punctual at his school. He was a mediocre student, shy and slow to mix with others. Many years later, he recalled his past, saying 'my intellect must have been sluggish and my memory raw'. During his school days, he never told a lie to his teachers or others. He was greatly influenced by an ancient play *Shravana Pitribhakti* portraying the boundless love of Shravan for his parents. Therefore, obedience to parents became Mohan's motto. Further, a play about Harischandra influenced him to lead a truthful and sincere life. From early boyhood, his young mind was experiencing a kind of spiritual bewilderment and groping which led him to try to read and understand *Manusmriti* which was almost his father's collection.

Gandhiji married Kasturba at the age of thirteen, while he was still in school. She was the daughter of a Porbander merchant, a friend to Gandhi family. By nature, Kasturba was quiet and self-possessed.

Gandhiji passed the matriculation in 1887 and joined the Samaldas College in Bhavnagar where he found the studies difficult and the atmosphere uncongenial. Right from his childhood, he was religious and used to recite *Ramanama* to overcome fear. After his father's death, he was offered to take up his father's place in the State service, but he wished that he would better become a Barrister. He was urged to study law in England. This was objected by his caste people. However, he pleaded for himself. His mother's objection to his going abroad was overcome by the son's solemn vow not to touch wine, women and meat. He was so determined on becoming a Barrister that even the formal excommunication from his caste would not deter him.

Gandhiji sailed for England in 1888. His initial days in England was miserable and he took time to accustom himself to the new situation. Later on he remarked, "I would continually think of my home and country... Everything was strange-the people, their ways and even their dwellings. I was a complete novice in the matter of English etiquette and continually had to be on my guard. There was the additional inconvenience of the vegetarian vow. Even the dishes that I would eat were tasteless insipid'.[2] While in England he read a book on *Plea for Vegetarianism* by Salt. This made him a vegetarian not only by his vow taken before his mother but also by principle. From then, the spread of the message of vegetarianism became a mission for him. His involvement with the vegetarians made him more sociable and popular. He was introduced to one poet, Narayan Hemachandra. On his request, he began to teach English. He undertook the task of becoming an English gentleman, but maintained the disciplined life of a student.

Gandhiji came across Theosophists who told him about *Bhagavad Gita*. Later in his life, *Gita* became a book of his daily reading. Once he said, 'When doubt hangs me, when disappointment stares me in the face and when I see not one ray of light on the horizon, I turn to the *Bhagavad Gita*, and find verse to comfort me and I immediately begin to smile in the midst of overwhelming sorrow'.[3] To him, the central theme of the *Gita* was that a balanced state of mind can be achieved by killing all passions and by renouncing desires, rather than objects. From this he deduced that the result of selfless detachment must be uttermost truth and non-violence. He believed that the *Gita* advocated the supremacy of moral power over physical force.

Gandhiji started reading the *Bible* and took great interest in the New Testament, particularly the Sermon on the Mount. He was attracted by the teaching of Buddha through Edwin's Arnold's *The Light of Asia*. A friend recommended Carlyle's *Heroes and Hero Worship,* which afforded him to know about Prophet Mohammed.

Gandhiji returned to India after the legal education in England. He decided to start his practice in Bombay, but could not make headway. Then he made efforts to establish himself as a lawyer in his native place, Rajkot. It was, at this juncture, that an offer came from Dadda Abdullah to proceed to South Africa on their behalf to instruct their counsel in a law suit. Thus, in April 1893, he sailed for South Africa without his family. He left for Pretoria, Capital of Transvaal, where his presence was required in connection with the case. It was in South Africa that the shy, timid, inexperienced and unaided Mohandas came into clash with the forces that obliged him to tap his hidden moral resources and turn the misfortune into creative spiritual experiences. He came face to face with racial prejudices and other oppressive atmosphere. Indians were treated as slaves and servants.

On his way to Pretoria, from Durban, at Maritzberg railway station,

Gandhiji was detrained from the first class compartment even though he was holding appropriate ticket. The train strode away and he was left alone on the platform. It was winter and severe cold. In that sleepless night, he determined to fight the indiscrimination and root out the social evils and suffer any amount of hardship. He decided to work for removing the racial discrimination and subordinated his legal practice to public work.

Regarding the legal issue for which he was summoned to South Africa, Gandhiji could successfully bring both the parties together for arbitration and he realised that the true function of a lawyer was to unite the parties driven apart. Bitter experiences of indignity and humiliation aroused the sense of social justice in him. He called for a meeting of Indian community in Pretoria and exhorted his countrymen to forget all distinctions of religion and caste and work for the welfare of the people. He also hinted to the miseries and problems caused by the discriminatory attitude of the English people and exhorted the need for ending such a treatment.

Gandhiji was about to sail back home when Natal Government proposed to introduce a Bill to defranchise Indians in South Africa. Heeding to the request of the Indians, he extended his stay in South Africa and enrolled himself as an advocate of the Supreme Court of Natal. During this time, he came under the influence of the book *Kingdom of God is Within You,* written by Tolstoy. Tolstoy pleaded for the refusal of military service and payment of taxes, rejected the concept of state and for the establishment of a non-violent society which is economically and politically decentralised. Though incidental, the reading of Ruskin's *Unto this Last* in 1904 had tremendous influence in his life. The magic spell of this book made Gandhiji to put his theories into practice. He founded Phoenix settlement near Durban and Tolstoy farm. He translated Ruskin's and Plato, loved to quote Thoreau, admired Mazzini, read Edward Carpenter and in short, was familiar with the best intellectual knowledge of Europe and America. He, who was 'Vaishnav' by birth, developed his gospel of *Ahinsa* as the spirit of his religion. The influence of the *Upanishads* on him is also worthy of study. He read Max Muller's translation of the *Upanishads* for the first time in 1894 in South Africa.

The Boer War broke out in 1889. As a matter of duty and patriotism, Gandhiji advised the Indian community to support the British corps. In 1901, he attended the Calcutta Session of the Indian National Congress and was satisfied over the resolution of South Africa. During the Zulu Rebellion in 1906, he stood loyal to British Empire and organized an Indian Ambulance Corps. He was happy that he and his men had to nurse the sick and dying Zulus whom the white doctors and nurses were unwilling to touch. During this period, he took the vow of *brahmacharya*, as he felt that true service to humanity could not be done honestly and sincerely unless one takes the life of *brahmacharya*.

Gandhiji introduced the non-violent but powerful revolutionary weapon called *Satyagraha* in response to the Black Act. The immigrants gave an ultimatum to General Smuts to repeal the Act before August 1908. In the absence of a positive response from General Smuts, certificates were burnt and Indians were now prepared to face imprisonment. All these events enabled the personality development of Gandhiji.

On return from duty in connection with the Zulu Rebellion, Gandhiji came to know the Draft Ordinance published in the Transvaal Government Gazette. This Ordinance required all Indians to register with the authorities to surrender the old permits taking their finger and thumb impression. Every individual who failed to do so was to forfeit his right of residence in Transvaal. He formed a passive resistance association to oppose such a move.

Gokhale visited South Africa in 1911 and informed Gandhiji that the Union Government had promised to repeal the Black Act. Later, the Union Government went back on its promise which made the Indians more furious. Meanwhile, a judgment of Supreme Court ruled that only Christian marriages were legal in South Africa, thus turning at one stroke all Indian wedlocks as invalid. This issue prompted the women to come forward and join the struggle. The continuous struggle organised in the non-violent way bore its fruits when the issue was successfully settled.

Gandhiji finally returned to India in January, 1915, not as a lawyer but as a well-experienced organiser in the cause of social justice and equality. The experiences of political struggle in South Africa widened his mental horizon and field of activity, promising India a ray of hope for the supressed humanity. Between 1893 and 1914, he visited India occasionally and those visits helped to maintain the link with Indian leaders like Gokhale, Tilak, Ranade etc.

Gandhiji was essentially a man of religion. He was not religious in the ordinary sense in which religion is understood in India. It was religion based on truth and love. That is why religion for him became the basis of all his activities, it became his philosophy of life, it functioned as a source of strength in him. He made it clear that religion in its real sense could become the basis of friendship among all mankind. He considered different religions as the different roads going towards the same destination. On the basis of his own experience and study of different religions he came to the conclusion that all religions were true and based on the same principles of truth and love. He emphasised repeatedly that religions were not separating men from one another but rather for binding them.

After returning from South Africa, Gandhiji spent the first year in India touring all over the country and studying it with 'his ears open but his mouth shut'. In 1917, the first *Satyagraha* in India was launched at Champharan in Bihar State. The peasants were compelled by the landlords to cultivate indigo on 15 per cent of their lands and part with the whole crop for rent. He skillfully tackled the problem in a non-violent way. The Government appointed a committee in which Gandhiji was also a member. On recommendations of the committee, a Bill was passed in favour of the tenant-farmers. Thus, the success of his first *Satyagraha* was registered. This was followed by Ahmedabad Textile Mill Workers strike on bonus issue. He advised the workers to go on strike and he also stipulated certain conditions. The strike went on for 21 days. During the strike, he initiated his maiden fast for three days and his intervention had the desired effects. The issue was soon settled amicably through arbitration.

Gandhiji's next *satyagraha* was in Kheda district of Gujarat. Due to the failure of crops, the farmers demanded certain tax concessions. Many leaders of national eminence participated in this *satyagraha* and finally the government suspended the revenue assessment for the poor farmers. This *satyagraha* paved the way to awaken the political conscience and made the government to realise the potentials of mass movement.

In 1919, the Rowlatt Act was enforced. This induced Gandhiji to involve himself actively. This Act was opposed by many leaders. They observed *hartal* on 6th April, 1919. The *hartal* was peaceful and successful. The ill-feelings of the people disappeared and the movement became more widely spread.

Gandhiji ardently worked for the Hindu-Muslim unity. He elucidated its value and importance through his various articles in *Young India*. He categorically remarked that only harmonious relationship between the various classes and castes could lead to the national integration, solidarity and prosperity. His eminence dominated the Indian political horizon from 1920 onwards. He gave a new thrust to Indian National Congress and made the politicians more active and positive revolutionaries. Gradually women also started participating in the national movement. He bridged the gulf between the intelligentsia and the masses and widened the concept of *Swaraj*. He became one with the nation and hence his life could be unmistakably identified with the Indian history.

Under Gandhiji's leadership, the Congress decided to boycott the election to be held in 1920. At the same time, Congress launched non-cooperation movement for securing *Swaraj*. His exhortation had energised the people to be prepared for arrest, imprisonment or any other form of tortures for the cause of national freedom. However, the tempo of the movement was hampered in February 1922 due to the outbreak of violence in Chauri Chaura. Due to this incident, he suspended the civil disobedience movement. Taking advantage of the anti-climax, the British Government arrested him. In September 1922, he decided to wear loin-cloth in order to identify himself with the millions of poor in India.

Gandhiji was sent to jail for six years in Yeravada. The news of his arrest and imprisonment magnified his image and reputation. He was released from the jail in February 1924 on medical ground. In 1925, he started writing "The Story of My Experiments with Truth" through *Young India*. The spell of eleven vows came from Yeravada jail. Since 1925, he continued to devote more attention to the Hindu-Muslim problem. Till 1928, he extensively toured and propagated the Constructive Programme. Under the leadership of Gandhiji, the Congress, in 1928, demanded *Poorna Swaraj*.

Till 1930, the manufacture of salt was a government monopoly. A 24 day march to the beach at Dandi was organised against the salt-tax. On 6th April, 1930, Gandhiji picked up a lump of salt and broke the British law. He was arrested on 5th May, 1930, and Sarojini Naidu assumed the leadership. In 1931, he was released and an agreement known as Gandhi-Irwin Past was reached.

The First Round Table Conference was held in 1931. Gandhiji placed the demands of the Congress. When the British Government refused to accept the demands of the Congress, the civil disobedience movement was once again started. In 1932, the British Government proposed to introduce, in the Constitution of India, a separate electorate not only for the Muslims but for the 'Untouchables' (*Harijan*) as well, thereby causing a permanent vivisection of the Hindu community. He decided to fast unto death. On reaching an agreement replacing the separate electorate, he broke his fast. On 11th February, 1932, the first issue of *Harijan* was published. In September 1933, he visited Wardha. He tried to raise a fund for the *Harijan*. In May 1934, Congress was permitted by the Government to meet at Patna. He severed his official connection with the Congress and he wanted to devote his time to constructive work which was meant to achieve and maintain *Swaraj*.

By 1936, Gandhiji had almost settled in Sevagram. And therefore,

Sevagram became the headquarters for his activity. From 1937 onwards, the communal disharmony increased between Hindu and Muslim. Discontentment frequently discussed in all Congress session. He was deeply pained by the riots between these communities. He considered it as a threat against national integration and solidarity and therefore tried his best to bring communal harmony.

With the outbreak of Second World War, Gandhiji was dragged back into the political arena. In March 1939, he undertook a fast in protest against the breach of promise by Thakore Saheb of Rajkot to the Praja Parishad which had been carrying on the struggle for responsible government in the state. Within a few days of his fast, Thakore Saheb agreed to fulfil the promise. By 1940, an anti-war campaign was launched. Vinoba, who led that movement was imprisoned soon. Despite his arrest, the campaign gained momentum.

Gandhiji once again left the Working Committee as he wanted to pursue his strategy of non-violence for independence and development. He did not want India to become independent under the shadow of war while the extremist members of Congress were less considerate towards the non-violent means of achieving independence.

In 1942, the British Cabinet sent the Cripps Mission to India with the new constitutional proposal. Gandhiji adopted uncompromising attitude towards the proposals of the Cripps Mission because those proposals did not satisfy the demands of the Congress. Gradually national feeling aroused against British rule and got crystallised in their demand that 'Britain must abandon her hold on India'. With clear conscience, he prepared the Quit India campaign for the complete withdrawal of British from India. The Quit India resolution was passed by AICC in August 1942. He addressed the Congress Committee in which he eloquently and emotionally propounded the slogan of 'Do or Die'. On 9th August, 1942, he was arrested and the Congress Committee was declared as unlawful organisation. His arrest led the mob burst into violence campaign and sabotage. He was more and more aggrieved and maintained that conquest policy should be unequivocally non-violent. Later, he resorted to 21 days fast.

In September 1945, Gandhiji went to Bombay with Pyarelal to meet Jinnah in order to find out a solution for united India. Jinnah was adamant for a separate nation for Muslim. Nehru's intervention in this regard was also without success. The Muslim League decided to celebrate 16th August 1946 as 'Direct Action Day'. It witnessed a powerful outbreak of communal rioting. Gandhiji was deeply shocked. He felt his dream of

Swaraj was dwindling. Yet he decided that all energies that he possessed should be thrown for the service of the people. He proceeded to Naokhali to hide himself in East Bengal until such time as the Hindus and Muslims learn to live together in peace and harmony. This ambition was to wipe out every tear from every eye.

Setting aside all other affairs, Gandhiji devoted himself whole-heartedly to his mission by holding prayer meetings, preachings to the people on fearlessness and the need for truth and non-violence. By the second week of March 1947, he left Naokhali and reached Patna. In Bihar, he did the same as in Naokhali. By then, British Government realised that there is no way out than giving freedom for India. It appointed a committee and proposed for an 'Interim Government' for India. On 22nd March, 1947, Lord Mountabatten flew to India and immediately invited Gandhiji to come to Delhi.

Gandhiji desired an undivided free India, but due to the indomitable attitude adopted by the communal groups, partition became inevitable. On the day of Independence and partition, there were communal disturbances in some pockets of the country like Bengal, Bihar and Punjab. Though India became independent on 15th August, 1947, Gandhiji was not happy over the communal riots and tension mounting in various parts of the country. He spent the day on fasting and spinning. He could not rest even after attainment of freedom. He felt that his words had ceased to be cared. He observed that the Congress was being corrupted by power. As such he wanted its dissolution and convert it as 'Lok Sevak Sangh'.

Though Gandhiji ardently worked for the Hindu-Muslim unity, his effort was misunderstood. The Hindu extremists were not ready to appreciate the success of his fast and they felt that Gandhiji had pledged the Hindu conscience to appease the Pakistanis. On the second day of the fast, an attempt was made on his life by throwing bomb. Though he escaped, he was not moved, but continued his discourse.

On 30th January, 1948, at one prayer meeting, Gandhiji was assassinated by a Hindu, Godse. He fell down on the ground uttering the words *'Heh Ram'*. Thus, the apostle of non-violence had fallen a victim to violence. On the Evening of 31st Jaunuary, 1948, his body was reduced to ashes on the banks of Jamuna. The sad news of his assassination was conveyed to the country by Jawaharlal Nehru over the All India Radio. He remarked, 'The light has gone out of our lives and there is darkness everywhere. Our beloved leader, Bapu as we call him, the father of our nation, is no more. The light has gone out, I said, and yet I was wrong. For the light that shone in this country was no ordinary light. The light that has illuminated this country for these many years will illumine this country for many years and a thousand years later that light will still be seen in this country and the world will see it and it will give solace to innumerable hearts.'[4]

II

Due to his discipleship and a close association with Gandhiji, the life and work of Vinoba has been inevitably linked with Gandhian thought. Vinoba himself never got tired of paying tribute to Gandhiji for shaping his life. However, a closer look at his thought reveals that he was an independent thinker in his own right. While Gandhiji was concerned with the independence of India, Vinoba attempted to shape the destiny of post-independence India.

Vinoba was born on 11th September, 1895 at Gagode. Gagode is a small village in the Pena Taluka of Colaba district of Maharashtra. The childhood of Vinoba was spent in this village upto the age of ten. He received his early education at home. His father Narhari was in government service at Baroda. Shambhurao was his grandfather. He was deeply religious and devout, spending most of his time in *Bhajan* and worship. Vinoba was greatly influenced by his grandfather. He had the golden opportunity of learning his first lessons in social reform and religious tolerance from his noble grandfather. Shambhurao's thinking was original and temperament liberal. On important festivals, he threw the temple open even to the *Harijans* of the town. Such an act on his part, doubtless required great courage in those days. He had offered a feast even to sweepers and chamars and himself served them with meals.

Shambhurao's wife, Gangabai, grandmother of Vinoba, was a very able and determined lady. She managed to learn reading and writing at the age of 55. She possessed a genial sense of humour and would face family troubles with courage and fortitude. Vinoba's father, Narhari was the eldest son. Rukminibai was his mother. They had five children. Vinoba was the eldest. His father was very scrupulous, methodical and disciplined in his behaviour. He was an admirer of western science and education and had the credit of producing the first *Khaki* cloth which was later used for the uniforms of the British soldiers. He obtained his Diploma from the Kala Bhavan in Baroda and worked for some time in the dyeing department of the Buckingham Mills. Later, he shifted to Baroda and served in the office of the government as a senior typist-clerk. He observed strict punctuality in all his activities and possessed a keen sense of cleanliness. He was deeply interested in researches and experiments in evolving a variety of colours for cloth-printing. He desired Vinoba to read English and French and proceed to foreign countries. He wrote several books on various aspects of Indian music.

Like Vinoba, his two brothers, Balkoba and Shivaji have remained Brahmacharis and devoted their lives to study and social service. Vinoba's early character was moulded mainly at the hands of his pious and affectionate mother. She led a life of simplicity, self-restraint and observed religious vows with regularity. She was so considerate to the so-called untouchables and always helped them in various ways. She encouraged Vinoba not to marry and remain a celebate throughout his life. She was so engrossed in singing devotional *Bhajans.* She always asked her sons to shed fear of all kinds and harbour unfailing faith in *Ramanama*. She was a devotee of Lord Shiva. Vinoba used to read out the Marathi daily *Kesari* to his mother in order to keep her in touch with current events. She was keen to understand the *Gita* as well. She had a deep faith in the grace of God that she would invariably recite *Ramanama* while mixing leaven with milk for turning it into curds.

Vinoba was a voracious reader. But he read nothing that he did not digest and enjoy. He was also quite fond of newspapers. His father taught him English, Mathematics etc for three years. In 1910, he began regular school life as a student of the fourth english standard. In the beginning he fared very creditably in his class tests and examinations. He was fond of Mathematics. It is the exactness of Mathematics which has become a part and parcel of his life. After passing his Matriculation in November 1913, he joined the Intermediate course. But he was not content with his life and ever since 1911 was thinking of leaving home for good and giving himself up to something higher.

Vinoba founded a Students' Society. This Mandal celebrated all festivals which fostered national consciousness. He was the central figure in this Mandal. His sharp intellect and forceful oratory had cast a spell over all. He makes people his own and so, once a person is attached to him in a bond of affection, the relationship stays for life. As an adolescent he was very hot-tempered and sarcastic. However, he was generally a happy-go-lucky person. He never paid any attention to his dress or haircut. He could easily walk 5 to 7 miles at a stretch. On an average he used to walk about 15 miles a day.

On 25th March, 1916, Vinoba was on the train to Bombay with friends, for appearing the Intermediate examination. He got down at Surat and took the train for Varanasi. He stayed in Varanasi for 2-3 months. He stayed in a small room on the banks of Ganga, ate from an alms' centre. The whole day was for reading and contemplation. He followed the traditional method of studying Sanskrit through Veda, Vedanga. He used to attend debates. In Baroda, he had read Gandhiji's famous speech delivered on the Foundation day of Banares Hindu University. The vigorous speech of Gandhiji had deeply impressed him. Vinoba met Gandhiji for the first time in the Kocharab Ashram in Ahmedabad. Vinoba became an inmate of the Ashram.

To quote Vinoba, 'Whether Gandhiji was subjecting me to his scrutiny, I know not. But according to me, I had tested him thoroughly and had I found him wanting, I could not have carried on with him. If he found, or would have later noticed, any number of deficiencies in me, he would still have kept me with himself. But as far as I am concerned, had I noticed any short-coming or deficiency in his faith in Truth, I could not have stayed there at all'.[5] In this way, the many-sided activities of Vinoba's Sadhana started. Meanwhile he felt the need for a year's change, for reasons of health as well as for further studies. He took a years's leave and went to Wai.

Vinoba returned to the Ashram, on the expiry of his one year's leave and joined the Ashram work. He did spinning, weaving, carding, etc. He used to enter deep into every job that he took up. A school was started in the Ashram. Vinoba was appointed to deliver religious discourses in this school. He taught Sanskrit and Mathematics. Gandhiji asked him to speak in the daily prayers on the *Gita.* Tilak attracted Vinoba from early age. He had very little direct contact with Tilak but the inner contact was deep and firm. His contribution to the Satyagraha Ashram was immensely important.

Gandhiji started a branch of the Satyagraha Ashram at Wardha. He sent Vinoba with all the responsibilities for the Ashram. Vinoba conducted various experiments in Ashram life. He took the Ashram to be an experiment-oriented institution. He insisted on strict observance of self-discipline and demanded compliance with the Ashram rules. Once Gandhiji sent him to Vykom village in Travancore to guide a *Satyagraha.* He did it well. Under the leadership of Vinoba, such *Sadhana* went for two and a half or three decades. It covered experiments in various fields such as Spinning, Weaving, Nai Talim, Cow-service, Leper service, etc. Vinoba and his colleagues engaged themselves fervently to evolve the entire science and art of Khadi. *Nai Talim, Goseva, Kushta-seva* and other activities developed during this period and Vinoba trained devoted and life-long experts in each of these fields. He was laying great stress on self-restraint in Ashram life.

The Ashram atmosphere was constantly one of work as well of the trinity—*Bhakti, Jnan* and *Vairagya.* All work was done in the spirit of worship. In 1938, Vinoba had grown very weak due to hard labour and numerous experiments. Gandhiji asked him to look after his health and go for a change of climate. Vinoba decided to go and live in Pavanar. He spent his time serene and happy.

Vinoba linked *khadi* with the basic problem of rural unemployment. He set up a labour centre in Nalwadi, with a teacher. Whoever sought employment, could join the centre, learn spinning and earn his livelihood. Jamnalal Bajaj and others wanted that Vinoba's ideas should be placed before the people. The Ashram started a monthly *'Maharashtra Dharma'* edited by Vinoba, which later became a weekly. Efforts were made for the removal of untouchability. As a result, the Laxminarayana temple at Wardha was thrown open to *Harijans* as far back as 1928. In 1930, a campaign for prohibition yielded the result that 15 to 16 thousand toddy trees were cut off.

Totally Vinoba was arrested six times and served sentences for 5-½ years in jail. He liked many aspects of jail life and said that 'real Ashram life can be lived and experienced only in jail. Counted clothes, a water-tumbler and a pot, these are all the utensils here. What else can go with the vow of non-accumulation. Timely bath, food, sleeping and walking. A very regular life. No freedom even to fall ill. The food is all along and every day tasteless. Do we observe more discipline in the Ashram? We will have to introduce all these for improving Ashram life'.[6] His deep thinking, meditation and contemplation continued in the jail. Some valuable literature was created here. When he was in Nagpur jail, he wrote the *Swarajya Shashtra* and prepared an anthology of *Marathi Bhajans* from Saint Jnaneswar, Eknath and Namdev. From Seoni Jail, he produced *Ishavasyavriti* and *Sthita-prajna-darshan.* In the last jail-term, he was pondering over the idea of 'release from all institutions' i.e. serving all institutions without being bound up with any. He also wanted to identify himself with those who lived on manual labour.

When Vinoba left home, he had a desire to go to the Himalayas, and also keeness to go to Bengal. Apparently he reached neither; but Vinoba says: 'Mentally, I reached both simultaneously. In Gandhiji, I found the tranquillity of Himalayas and also the revolutionary fervour of Bengal. The line of thinking I got there was a unique combination of both Revolution and Absolute tranquillity. I got much from Gandhiji's Ashram; as a consequence, I experienced that life is identical and integrated. After entering the Ashram, I could perceive this; I got my eyes as it were.

Gandhiji's Ashram is my alma mater which gave me this insight'. Regarding Vinoba, Gandhiji says, "He is one of the rare jewels of the Ashram. He has come to purify the Ashram with his own religious merit; he has come not to receive but to give."[7]

After Gandhiji's assassination two or three years passed in the search for the path. In March 1948, there was a conference of the country's constructive workers at Sewagram. It was mainly due to Vinoba's inspiration that the Sarvodaya Samaj and later Sarva Seva Sangh, were started. At Jawaharlal's request, he agreed to spend 6 months, on an experimental basis, in helping to rehabilitate persons belonging to the Mewa Tribe from Delhi, Punjab and Rajasthan.

Vinoba spread the message of love and goodwill in the atmosphere of communal narrow-mindedness. His truthfulness, spirit of devotion and deep study of all religions wielded a tremendous influence. He was invited by the Muslims to accompany them to the Dargarh-Shareef and offer prayers. There he offered the common inter-religious prayers. He travelled to other places in the country and tried to create a climate of communal harmony and equal respect for all religions.

After about 21 months of nation-wide travels, Vinoba returned to the Ashram. In the meantime, he had seen that even though the country had attained political independence, Gandhiji's chief mission was still incomplete. The incomplete work of Gandhiji was to be advanced mainly through freedom from economic exploitation and freedom from political bondage. Vinoba started a vigorous campaign for freedom from wealth. All commodities required for living, should be produced by manual labour in the Ashram itself, to the extent possible. This was a unique experiment of labour-based living.

The Sarvodaya conference was to be held at Shivarampalli in Andhra Pradesh. Vinoba agreed to attend it at the insistence of his friends. He started his journey on foot from Sevagram on 7th March, 1951. In thirty days, he walked about 300 miles to reach the place. In the presence of all the constructive workers, he said, 'The mission to be achieved after independence is very profound indeed and also difficult. The task is to function as foundation stones of society. We have to take up now the work of social and economic revolution'. For every worker, he propounded a five-point programme - inner purification, external cleanliness, manual labour, tranquillity and dedication. At the end of the conference, he announced that he would like to see for himself the conditions in Telangana through a journey on foot. He started his journey on 15th April 1951. He visited communist prisoners in the jail at Hyderabad. He talked to them with deep sympathy.

On 18th April, 1951, Vinoba reached Pochampalli on foot. He went round the village. The Harijans in the village asked him for help. He went into deep thought, as he could not see any way out. Mr. Ramachandra Reddy came forward to donate 100 acres of land. Vinoba was overwhelmed. In this way *Bhoodan* was started. That night, he could not sleep for three to four hours. He went on asking, and people went on giving. On 27th June he returned to Pavanar. Till then, 12000 acres of land were received in *Bhoodan* in 70 days. In Pavanar, he got busy with the experiment on the programme for freedom from wealth. He had no idea of going out again soon thereafter.

Jawaharlal Nehru invited Vinoba to come to Delhi and have detailed discussions with himself and with the Planning Commission. Vinoba accepted the invitation and decided to undertake a *Padayatra*. He stayed in Delhi for 10 days. He had detailed discussion with Nehru as also with the Planning Commission. He almost challenged the Planning Commission. He said, 'If, besides heavy industries, you have any other programmes which could provide work to everyone in the country, I would set fire to *Charkha* and not shed a tear. But I am sure that without the help of *charkha* and the village industries, you cannot provide work to the entire population of India. You accept the responsibility to plan for reaching the target. So I have to say that your planning is not for the entire country but for merely a certain section of it'.[8] He had presented the essential outlines of planning according to Gandhian way of thinking. His thinking was absolutely clear.

From Kanyakumari to Kashmir, thousands and lakhs of acres of land were received in donation. Land, for which people ruin themselves in litigation or commit murders and blood-shed, was offered by people, with love. Thousands donated lakhs of acres for distribution to their own landless brothers. In all 42 lakh acres of land was received and 15 lakhs were actually distributed. His march continued and reached new dimensions. From land-gifts came the idea of *Gramdan* in Mangroth. The Mangroth people offered the entire land in their village to him. From such an incident, the idea of village-gift arose. The village-gift idea gave a new direction to the *Bhoodan* movement.

In 1953, there was a Sarvodaya conference at Chandil. At Chandil, Vinoba proclaimed, 'We have to generate people's strength and arouse it, as opposed to the power of violence and different from the power of Government. Violence, in fact, will not be of use. Our work is to create conditions in the country in which there is no occasion to apply the sanction of law, which we have entrusted to the Government. This people's power is not opposed to the power of law — but is different from it. All our work should be geared towards ultimately bringing about the condition of non-dependence on governmental authority for punishment'.[9] On listening to this Chandil address, Jayaprakash Narayan exclaimed, 'I have become a devotee of Vinoba'. In the 1954 Bodhgaya Conference, Jayapraksh Narayan offered his lifelong service to this cause.

During his Bengal tours in 1963, Vinoba put forth the idea of *gramdan* as a comprehensive programme of village self-rule. The ownership of land was to vest in the village society, as in the original concept. The second step of *gramdan* was to lay down the rule that the land-holders in these villages were to donate 1/20th of their holding for the landless. The third matter about *gramdan* was that while everyone will produce or earn something on his land, he will give 1/40th of it annually to the village society. Non-cultivators will give their one day's earnings every month. Labourers will offer their labour for a day every month. In this manner, *gramdan* became an efficient and well-planned programme of village *Swarajya*. It achieved a coordination of individual freedom and dedication to society, a perfect balancing of freedom and equality. He explained time and again that a village — family cannot be constituted until *gramdan* is obtained. Without it there is no solid foundation for our comprehensive work.

Alongwith *gramdan,* Vinoba suggested several other programmes necessary for building up a Sarvodaya society. He continued to lay emphasis on the Shanti-Sena programme. He used to speak of taking Khadi production programme to the village and said that Khadi was directly linked with economic independence as well as with village self-rule. Once Jayaprakash Narayan said, 'After Gandhiji, if any single name in the entire world has given a ray of hope, it is that of Vinoba. His activities like *Bhoodan, Gramdan* and *Shanti Sena* have drawn the attention of the whole world. With programmes like Bhoodan, he has started a stupendous effort to introduce spiritual values in collective social life. The most important index of the development of a society is the development of its human qualities. Vinoba's programmes offer a solution to the problem of building up a new society, on the basis of ethical values. Vinoba's movement is a great experiment of human development as well as of social reconstruction. That is why the entire world looks up to him'.[10]

Vinoba had an idea firmly fixed in his mind, that Sarvodaya cannot be brought about if we become only a Naradmuni. He was also sure that one could not bring about a change in government's attitude just somehow. The Bihar campaign was nothing but a stupendous effort to secure people's consent for Sarvodaya idea. In the Rajgir conference, Vinoba declared many matters relating to the future line of work. He said, 'So far we were after this programme with a single mindedness, which some would regard a defect. Now we have completed one stage. So we should add a few more matters. We must start work in cities also mainly for two or three purposes. We have to liberate municipalities from party - politics; that should not enter there. Next, we have to organise each *mohalla* as a Shanti-Sena Centre. For raising a Shanti Sena for the whole city, a well-thoughtout plan will have to be prepared. Thirdly, we have to explain to the labour class not to associate their trade unions with any party. Otherwise, their interests tend to get neglected and political interests achieve their own purpose. Moreover, special efforts should be made to draw labour towards Sarvodaya ideology. Fourthly, in cities it would not be enough if the millionares and industrialists give a little in donation. We should try that they accept their full social responsibility. We should put up such a demand, and should develop such strength that the demands are not ignored or refused'.[11]

From 1951 onwards, for about 25 years, there was an experiment on country-wide scale for introducing Gandhian ideology in the socio-economic field. It was proved that land could be obtained by compassion instead of by blood-shed or by force of law. In 1963 Vinoba said, 'I had formerly thought that after donating his land, the donor had no further right to interfere in its distribution. This was a grave mistake. It occurred due to false pride of bringing about a revolution, and presumption of virtuous merit in doing so. Instead if it had been then decided that the donor could himself distribute his land, much more land would have been promptly distributed and a bond of love would have developed between donor and donee'.[12]

The word *Bhoodan* was born in 1951 and the *Gramdan* idea occurred in 1952. Its new form was put before the public in 1963. A glimpse of its potentiality to become extensive was seen by 1969. The thought and feeling agitated the public at large. A philosophy of Sarvodaya took shape and it became clearer that *Hind Swaraj* would be meaningful only in *Gram-Swaraj*. While Vinoba was in the Ashram, solitary *Sadhana*, profound experiments and silent service were the main features. He remained permanently attached to the freedom movement and the various constructive programmes. He watched all the events in the country, including political ones. He thought that evading social problems did not give peace to the mind.

For Vinoba, the idea of national integration became a strong reality.

National integration can be visualised only when : 1. the entire population could be aroused by a common sentiment, 2. when they could feel the vibrations of a common experience simultaneously, and 3. when they could revere a number of great men reflecting the entire nation in themselves.

He delivered about 17000 talks in the *Yatra* and another 3000 elsewhere, that is, altogether about 20,000 talks. His speech flowed ceaselessly like the Ganga. After independence Vinoba put before all the workers the new goal of Sarvodaya. He initiated them to Sarvodaya ideology. He made them personally give up their selfish attitudes and think in terms of social good. He drew them to purer and nobler joy and cultivated their entire approach to life in his own inimitable way. He trained all his workers to be all-India servant. He was deliberately trying to educate these workers to develop their independent thinking also. He laid stress on meditation and studies.

In 1960, during the march, a sacred event took place. Twenty-one dacoits came and surrendered themselves, as if violence was surrendering its arms before non-violence. Vinoba handed over to the Police the dacoits who had surrendered. In 1959, Vinoba travelled in Kashmir. On entering Kashmir he said, 'God willing, I wish to do three things, — to see, to hear and to love. I wish to apply here all the power of love, which God has given me. If I am found wanting, I will ask for more strength from Him. If I have to speak, I will speak only for this and will not speak more'. In Kashmir, he wandered a lot, mixing freely with the common men. He went into deep and remote villages where few outsiders reach. There also he met people in their homes and enquired about their difficulties.

In September 1962, Vinoba had his journey on foot for 16 days in East Pakistan. He used to hold silent prayers there, as he often did in India in very large gatherings. In 1962, our borders had to face Chinese aggression. He was then touring in the interior of Bengal. His attitude provided correct guidance to the country in the troubled times of Chinese aggression. His non-violence is discriminating in many ways, such as discrimination between justice and injustice, discriminating about our limitations of the development of *ahimsa,* discrimination of not opposing traditional measures for achieving what *Ahimsa* cannot at present achieve and discrimination to apply oneself wholly to strengthening the power of Ahimsa.

Vinoba started a movement to remove obscene posters. His remarks on unbecoming posters are absolutely logical. He said, 'I am not against cinema, I advocate scientific progress. I desire that we should have good films and I am not raising a cry against even bad ones as yet. To stop that would require public opinion. A demand for better censorship could also be raised. While people pay for seeing films in a cinema-house, the posters are displayed on public roads, they naturally occur to every one. Sometimes they are so ugly that a good person cannot even bear their sight. Thus, this constitutes an aggression on public liberty. They leave a very bad impression on tender minds, for children they provide free and compulsory education on sex-indulgence. What is obscene may be decided by a committee of known and reputed citizens. For sisters, it becomes a programme to protect their modesty.'[13]

In 1965, there was a holocast in the country on the question of language. The Prime Minister and the Chief Ministers of all States accepted Vinoba's Three-point formula — there should be no violence; Hindi should not be imposed on those who want English to stay; English should not be imposed on those who want Hindi.

Vinoba always stressed purity of heart and discard of ego. When a person is completely egoless and when he is completely dedicated, his action, thought and meditation draw limitless strength. He has reached a firm conviction that narrow-mindedness cannot solve the problems confronting humanity—problems of language, religious sects, national boundaries, commerce and trade, exploitation and so on — all very often problems of our attachment to the body. They are based on narrow-mindedness.

In October 1970 Vinoba said that he had received an inner direction for confining himself to Pavanar. Naturally he gave up all other fields of work. He observed silence for a year from December, 1974. On 25th December, 1976, he announced complete freedom from all activity. He relinquished responsibility for the direct work of the movement. He said that he would no longer go to the people, but will offer advice to those who come to him naturally. In short, he went on reducing external activity as far as possible so that the distraction from the special experience of entering the abstract may be gradually minimised.

On 7th June 1970, Vinoba moved to Brahma-vidya Mandir. Now he had given up direct activity in society, but was not opposed to social contacts. Through his abstract meditation and *'abhidhyan'* he was advising and guiding people who came to him, and thus he was trying to keep his activities to the minimum possible. Adding *Nagari Script* and *Brahma Vidya* to the existing programmes of *Gramdan, Shantisena* and *Acharya Kula,* he gave to the workers a five point programme. He said that for carrying out this programme we have to secure the cooperation of five powers.

Regarding the cooperation of five powers Vinoba said, 'These five powers are like our five fingers. The first is the thumb, which is sturdy; it stands for people's power. It has to stand on the strength of *ahimsa* and *satya.* The second one is the small finger the inner urge - which stands for the power of good man. In simple words, it is the power of the Sevaks, workers engaged in life-long service on the basis of moral principles like truth, while themselves living on the strength of these principles. The third finger is index finger-which points to the correct way; this stands for the power of scholars. The scholars have to guide all, while keeping themselves aloof; they study the events in the world disinterestedly and place their opinion before the world. The fourth is the power of the rich i.e. those engaged in business and industries - big and small. They also constitute a power, before whom Gandhiji placed the concept of trusteeship. This is the middle finger. The fifth finger is called the nameless one, *anamika.* People wear their rings in it and call it ring-finger as it has no particular work assigned to it. It has only to bring about coordination between all the powers; it stands for government power. Today it may have assumed supremacy but some day its importance will certainly diminish and it will remain a power in name only. Cooperation of all these powers will have to be secured by those who work in public.' [14]

In April 1974, with regard to Bihar unrest, Vinoba said, 'Corruption, inflation, unemployment, and educational changes - the planks on which the agitation has started - are all matters requiring consideration, not agitation. Who does not agree that there should be reforms in education? What can you get by agitating about it? What is required is careful consideration. Inflation is a question of money-economy, if we want to get rid of it, we have to attain as much 'freedom from markets' as possible. It will not to do say that Government alone is responsible for inflation. It may be feasible to set up a commission to examine the changes required in the election laws or in the Constitution. Moreover, there is the question of setting up candidates from rural areas. Corruption that prevails in other spheres is of many forms. How can you remove it by agitating? And if you just agitate for removing government, it will ultimately be an opposition of democracy itself'.[15]

What Vinoba wanted to say was that today the world has become so small that even the politics of this country should be viewed in the context of the world situation. The consequences of each step should be correctly weighed. The main problem now-a-days is that the country is breaking up. Therefore, we should work as a cementing factor. Otherwise, the country's unity will be in danger. Our country is surrounded by dictatorial neighbours. If the Central Government falls in such circumstances it may not be able to recover. If any such situation arises there are numerous countries, big and small, waiting for the opportunity to benefit from it. Indiraji's foreign policy is firm and wise. She may have committed many serious blunders in internal matters. This also raises many important questions indeed. But attempt should be made to solve all of them through negotiation. This will maintain a climate of cooperation and goodwill in the country. Our role should be to bring people together, not to disrupt them.

On 26th June, 1975, National Emergency was proclaimed. Jayaprakash Narayan and others were sent to jail. Vinoba was observing silence during the period. His first reaction was that the Emergency was an outcome of the charming going on in the country for a year or two. He imagined that it will be used only as an adhoc shock treatment. But later the real situation unfolded itself to him gradually and the true nature of Emergency also became clearer. In the form of a maxim, he had mentioned in July that this was an 'Occasion for discipline' and once or twice, he had also expounded its implications which however were not made public. Therefore, the maxim was much misused by Government and led to a good deal of undeserved misunderstanding about Vinoba. His clear exposition became public only much later on 25th December when his one year's silence ended.

In 1976, Vinoba had announced his fast to begin on 11th September, if cow-slaughter was not banned in the entire country: Government applied the censor's whip and did not allow even this decision to be published. Vinoba remarked, 'What cowards have we become? Our press would not publish such a pious resolution because of Government censorship. Supposing tomorrow I pass away during the fast and Government declares that Vinoba died of heart-failure, will you all publish it that way? Government can arrest and bind you, even send you to jail. It can do nothing more. But if you have courage, they cannot harm you. God helps those who help themselves. Everyone should fearlessly go to the temple and say what one considers correct and proper. Not moving underground but openly, you must place before people your views and thoughts, whether about the Emergency or about cow-slaughter. How many would they keep in jail?' After this, Government had a talk with him and announced that all the States would legislate about ban on cow-slaughter within a year or so.

During Emergency Vinoba was pondering a lot. He was searching for some non-violent panacea to solve the problem and create an atmosphere of mutual trust and goodwill in the country. He wanted that while all win no one loses; just as when India gained independence, the British gained the goodwill of Indians because they left without any rancour. But Vinoba found no such panacea nor did he get any inner direction. After the Emergency, the Sarva Seva Sangh met. He advised that the Sangh may be wound up. This however, did not happen, but his affection for the Sangh remained undiminished. He said that there were many good persons in the Sangh. Whenever his advice was sought, he gave it lovingly. His love for Jayaprakash Narayan continued as before. There was no change in their mutual relations; they were unaffected by the differences.

At the age of 84, Vinoba undertook a fast for securing a ban on cow-slaughter. After five days of fast, the Central Government announced that legislation in the light of the Supreme Court's decision will be taken up; necessary amendments in the Constitution will be made to put this subject on the concurrent list. Vinoba said, 'From a universal point of view, man should not exploit nature. Indian culture accepted the fact that man is also an indivisible part of nature, and as a consequence of experiments spread over thousands of years, included the cow and its progeny as family members of the human race. It is a fine example of the mutual relationship of animal and man. In the Indian economy the cow has the highest place; it is the pivot of rural economy. Only agriculture and animal husbandry have the potentiality to feed the sixty crores of our people. Indian agriculture is based on the bullok. Cowdung gives the best compost and Gobar-gas plant is the best source of energy.'[16]

Vinoba tried to find the dynamics of social change through non-violence and love. Never before was a serious effort directed towards this until Gandhiji's constructive programme made such an attempt. He carried out a large scale experiment on it. He says that *Satyagraha* is used now-a-days mainly for securing relief from the oppression of laws. But it is not an instrument of revolution. There is a place for *satyagraha* even in democracy, because *satyagraha* is a way of life and a way of conduct. At the same time in special situations it may also be a remedy.

Vinoba has expounded public morality in great detail. He has given some practical hints for immediate action and also some thoughts to bring about basic alterations. Unfortunately no one paid heed to him when he was spelling out a code of public morality, and pointing out some particular danger-spots in democracy as adopted by us from the West.

There are some fine instances of his sarcasm. He said, 'In the field of thought, you have more often to refute the theories of those nearer to you than of those more remote. Shankaracharya did not refute the atheists so much as he refuted *Sankhyavada*, which is closer to his theory. That is because what is close to us differs from us only in some small detail. Thus there is a greater probability of being misled. So the closest ideas have to be formulated and defended first. Later, it does become quite clear as to where the real point of difference is. When we turn to social work, the position is reversed. If you oppose the near ones in this, it would amount to driving them away. One has to keep this line of demarcation between social service and spiritual thought."[17]

Swarajya for Gandhiji and *Gram-swarajya* for Vinoba were not political objectives, but spiritual goals. Their concepts of *swarajya* are very much the same. Vinoba took the vow of celibacy and social service at the age of ten. Ever since, his mind has been fastened to one equation: *Swa-rajya* = our own kingdom = the kingdom of the soul. Years later, he wrote *Swarajya-shashtra*. Rajya is one thing, *swarajya* is quite another. You can get kingdom by violence. *Swarajya* is impossible without non-violence. Hence a thoughtful person will not desire a kingdom, but he pines for *swarajya*. *Swarajya* will mean every man's kingdom i.e. a kingdom which everyone regards as his own, in other words, the kingdom of all, or *Ramarajya*. He says in the *Samya-sutra*, 'you get freedom from government, when you realise your own soul power'.

Vinoba did not die a natural death. He invited it. If one carefully reads the various accounts, later made available, of his extraordinary decision and behaviour in the first fortnight of November 1982, one would not fail to notice that the idea of giving up voluntarily 'the *Holy Ghost*' probably first occurred to him on 7th November. It is difficult to say whether he had, before this, thought of discarding the age-worn and disease-ridden body specifically by abstaining from taking both food and water. He did not believe in dying of a disease. He wanted to die of starvation as a result of a deliberate decision. He had passed away on 15th November, 1982.

REFERENCES

1. Pyarelal, *Mahatma Gandhi : The Last Phase I*, NPH, Ahmedabad, 1956, p.74.
2. Mahajan P. Mani, *Foundations of Gandhian Thought*, Dattsons Publishers, Nagpur, 1987, p.3.
3. *Young India*, 20.12.1928.

4. Shah, K., *Vinoba on Gandhi*, SSS, Varanasi, 1973, p.66.
5. Vinoba, *Democratic Values*, SSS, Varanasi, 1962, p.18.
6. Shah, K., *Vinoba, Life and Mission*, SSS, Varanasi, 1967, p.79.
7. *Bhoodan Ganga*, Volume 2, p.33.
8. Vinoba, *Swarajya Shastra*, SSS, Varanasi, 1945, p.64.
9. Vinoba, From Bhoodan to Gramdan, *Sarvodaya Prachuralaya*, Tanjore, 1957, p.43.
10. Jaiprakash Narayan, *From Socialism to Sarvodaya*, SSS, Varanasi, 1961, p.48.
11. Tandon, V., *Sarvodaya After Gandhi*, SSS, Varanasi, 1976, p.89.
12. Sharma, J.S., *Vinoba and Bhoodan*, INC, New Delhi, 1969, p. 120.
13. Tandon, V., *Selections from Vinoba*, SSS, Varanasi, 1972, p.66.
14. Vinoba, Gram Swaraj, *Sarvodaya Prachuralaya*, Tanjore, 1962, p.23.
15. Nargolkar, V., *Crime and Non-violence*, S.R.G. Trust, Poona, 1974, p.86.
16. Nargolkar, V., *The Creed of Saint Vinoba*, Bharatiya Vidya Bhavan, Bombay, 1963, p.32.
17. Groom, D., *With Vinoba*, SSS, Varanasi, 1978, p.68.

2

PHILOSOPHICAL THOUGHT OF GANDHI AND VINOBA

Gandhiji's philosophy of truth and non-violence is primarily based on spiritual idealism and metaphysical assumptions. His belief in God, developed in his early life, continued to the end of his life and at the same time he could raise the value of truth of one's own experience to the highest degree. His mother was a great devotee of God. All thoughts and actions of him had their foundation in religion. The outstanding impression that his mother has left on his memory is that of saintliness. She was deeply religious. She would not think of taking her meals without her daily prayers. His father used to enjoy talks at home about different religions and had lengthy discussions with the people belonging to different religions.

Throughout his life, Gandhiji remained as a religious man. He believed that religion helped him to attain self-realisation. To him, God is an indefinable mysterious power that pervades everything. God is not only an unalterable and intelligent law, but the law of love, which is what makes him specially accessible through *ahimsa.* To the man, who has realised truth in its fullness, nothing else remains to be known, because all knowledge is necessarily included in it. What is not included in it is not truth and, so, not true knowledge. The meaning for God, to Gandhiji includes omnipotent, omniscient and omnipresent entity which exists. He did not mind calling God as a person, because personality was for him a symbol to express the transcendent reality. To him, God is life, God is love, God is law, God is light and God is liberation. God is not merely an over ruling power, but a benevolent one; for it ensures the persistence of value in the midst of disvalue. God is the architect of good, never of evil. He speaks of God as a living power that is changeless, that holds together, that creates, dissolves and recreates and as an unalterable law governing everything and every being that exists or lives.

Gandhiji identified God as symbol of supreme value. He found Him incarnate in every individual. He gave various descriptions to God. He said, 'To me God is truth and love; God is ethics and life, and yet He is above and beyond all these. God is conscience. He is a personal God to those who need his personal presence. He is embodied to those who need His touch. He is the purest essence. He is all things to all men. He is in us and yet above and beyond us'.[1] He also says that it is difficult to define God.

Moral discipline is essential for knowing God. Purity of heart is the important condition for feeling the presence of God. He said that the devotees who visit even the most unholy temples with pure heart certainly feel the presence of God in those temples. Moral and spiritual discipline enables one to experience self-realisation. God is proved by extraneous evidence but in the transformed conduct and character of those who have felt the real presence of God within. God is beyond the reach of the senses; we cannot truly define Him or prove His existence. God is both unprovable and indescribable. Man can only conceive God within the limitations of his own mind. Gandhiji calls God as 'the mystery of mysteries'. It is only through self-purification that one can create the right conditions for acquainting the presence of God.

According to Gandhiji, the manner is which a man's God consciousness is to be communicated to others must be similar to the way in which he has himself blessed with it. It is good and proper that when we feel satisfied that we have found God and that God has spoken to us, we should wish to share that mystery, but as God has spoken to us mysteriously, we should allow that God. Further, religion is like a rose. It throws out the scent which attracts us like a magnet and we are drawn to it involuntarily. The scent of religious contact has a greater pungency than the scent of the rose.

The individual should prepare themselves to realise God through prayer and self-discipline. Commitment is needed. To realise God, one should become a votary of truth, truth led one to see God face to face. Gandhiji urged on undergoing the discipline enjoined by the five vows of truth, non-violence, *brahmacharya,* non-possession and non-stealing to apprehend the Reality. To him, God is Truth in so far as He is an eternal and infinite Being. He calls the God as a Father. The man-God relationship is the only relation which can regulate all the aspects of human life. He calls the man-God relation as 'the Central experience of life'. This relation is central. No human activity has the right to ignore this relation. He underestimates the importance of reason. He opposes the need of reason.

The problem of good and evil is one of those arising from the thoughts about God. Regarding the problem of evil, Gandhiji said, 'I cannot account for the existence of evil by any rational method .... I am therefore humbly enough to recognise evil as such. And I call God long-suffering and patient precisely because He permits evil in the world. I know He has no evil in Him, and yet if there is evil, He is the author of it and yet untouched by it. I know too that I shall never know God if I do not wrestle with and against evil even at the cost of life itself.'[2] He openly admits his ability to explain the existence of evil in relation to God. The distinction between good and evil is our creation. *Yamas* and *Niyamas* are important for God-realisation. To realise God we have to become good ourselves. It is only as a result of continual self-discipline, rather than as extroverted seeking, that one can grow up into an experience of God.

> To quote R.R. Diwakar: "The concept of God by its very nature is bound to be dynamic as it evolves with the person or the group of persons who hold by the particular concept. It can be partially compared to the ideal of perfection. The nearer we approach the ideal of our perfection, the further it recedes and we are allured to follow it to eternity. Similarly, in the case of the concept of God, the more we think and feel that we have a full grasp of the concept of God, new vistas open us, because God is Infinite itself and there cannot be an end or a final concept. That is why the purer and deeper is the consciousness of the seeker of God, the mightier and nobler does the concept of God become. In fact, the concept of God in its very nature has to be a personal one and its evolution has to depend on the spiritual evolution of the person concerned. There cannot be any greater violence to the concept of God than institutionalising it and providing it with a straightjacket without complete freedom for individuals constituting the fraternity."[3]

Gandhiji came to know that there were so many persons who could deny the existence of God and also those who could not deny the existence of Truth. So, he considered 'Truth is God' as the highest value. God is Truth means truth is the only attribute of God ; Truth is one of the attributes of the God; Truth is the finest and the best attribute of God; God is truthful; God may be understood as clearly and logically as Truth is apprehended; God is to be known directly and intuitively like Truth, presupposing this particular method of arriving at Truth; God is appealing and acceptable as Truth; it is the clearest truth that God is; wherever God is; Apparently the idea of God is more important as God is the subject and Truth is the predicate and the predicate cannot exist without subject; Truth seems to be more important as God is explained or defined in terms of Truth; God is just the other name of Truth.

Truth is God means Truth is the only attribute of God; Truth is one of the attributes of God; Truth is the finest and the best attribute of God; Truth is as eternal as God; Truth is an object of respect and worship as God is; wherever Truth is, God is; Apparently the idea of Truth is more important as Truth is the subject and God is the predicate; it is a religious concept as Truth is defined in terms of God; Truth is just the other name of God.

In 1932, Gandhiji clearly explains the reason why he shifted from God is Truth to Truth is God. He said, "I would say with those who say God is Love, God is Love. But deep down in me I used to say that though God may be Love, God is truth, above all. If it is possible for the human tongue to give the fullest description of God, I have come to the conclusion that for myself, God is Truth . . . . I never found a double meaning in connection with truth and even atheists had not demurred to the necessity or power of truth. But in their passion for discovering the truth the atheists have not hesitated to deny the very existence of God—from their own point of view rightly. And it was because of such reasoning that I saw that rather than say that God is Truth, I should say that Truth is God".[4]

Gandhiji wanted to include every honest human being, even a denier of God, to march towards the great destiny of mankind, a destiny of peace, harmony and happiness, as is the trend of the urge of the evolution of man on earth. By declaring that Truth is God, he lifts us from our ancient mooring of the ism, theology and all that they mean by it, and ranks us afresh with every seeker of truth, with radical thinkers, with rationalists, and so on. To quote Sugata Dasgupta, "Gandhiji's entire approach was societal in content. Although Gandhi resposed great faith in God and believed in the values of spirituality and ethics, his spirituality, his God and his ethics were all products of the societal reality."

Prayer and worship are aiming towards the same goal, that is, to help one in realising one's self. Still a slight difference is there between prayer and worship. Prayer implies a humble request for the grant of a boon may be His grace, His help, or anything else that one thinks would make it possible for one to realise one's self. Worship consists in the expression of our adoration and love for God. Prayer means asking God for something in a reverent attitude. But the word is used also to denote any devotional act. It is a yearning of the heart to be one with the Maker, an invocation for His blessings. It is not an asking. It is longing of the soul. It is a daily admission of one's weakness. It is a felt relation between His surpassing greatness and One's own insignificance. It is the very soul and essence of religion and, therefore, prayer must be the very core of the life of man, for no man can live without religion.

Prayer is not to be performed with lips. Prayers of those whose tongues are nectared but whose hearts are full of poison are never heard. He therefore, who would pray to God, must cleanse his heart. A prayerful heart is the vehicle and service makes the heart prayerful. Prayer is an impossibility without a living faith in the presence of God within. We may pray to God for moral strength, wisdom, light, mercy or anything else. We awaken our soul from slumber. When the soul is awakened, or when we pass on from the sleeping state of the soul, to its real wakeful state, when we destroy ego. What we do or attempt to do—we feel our identity with the soul. The self is realised. Prayer is either petitional or in its wider sense is inward communion. In either case the ultimate result is the same. Even when it is petitional, it should be for the cleansing and purification of the soul, for freeing it from the layers of ignorance and darkness that envelop it.

Prayer is no mere exercise of words or of the ears, it is no mere repetition of empty formula. It is better in prayer to have a heart without words than words without a heart. Prayer has the ultimate aim of annihilating our ego and fixing our consciousness on the one indwelling soul. It is a continual effort to live in ever greater harmony with one's higher self. Gandhiji relates the prayer to truth. He said, "To propiliate the Truth is *Prarthana* which in effect means an earnest desire to be filled with the spirit of Truth. This desire should be present all the twenty-four hours. But our souls are too dull to have this awareness day and night. Therefore, we offer prayers for a short-time in the hope that a time will come when all our conduct will be one continuously sustained prayer."[5]

The object of prayer is union with God and what stands in the way of that union is our ego. In prayer we have to forget ourselves and by doing that we can gain our inner self. When we pray to God we are really praying to ourself. There are different methods of prayer and each and everybody has the right to select his own way. Humility is a must for prayer. The devotee should realise that the need for prayer is his, and not God's. Faith is the necessary pre-condition as well as the product of Prayer. We cannot pray unless we believe in God. Faith and prayer calls for increasing self-discipline. Both make for equanimity, self-purification and *ahimsa;* and of course both imply ever-growing closeness to and dependence on God. Faith in God is a necessary component of prayer.

The aim of prayer is to nourish the spirit. We can never achieve perfect purity. Our need for prayer is never quite met. Gandhiji openly subscribes to the idea that all things are really His, and that what seems to be ours has given to us only for custody and proper use. A man of prayer believes that God works in a mysterious way and wants the whole world to possess the truth he himself has seen. He would simply pray for it to be shared. God being perfect, does not need our prayer. Being 'all love' he would tolerate us all even if we do not pray. But if we feel, as we should that we owe a debt to Him who is the giver of all things. We should remember Him and pray to Him out of gratitude. Prayer makes us look within ourselves, and realise His immanence.

Prayer leads to self-purification. Prayer enables us to distinguish right from wrong, to resist evil, and above all to remain conscious of our duty towards our fellowmen. Prayer is necessary not only for our inner evolvement but also for facing bravely everyday challenges in our life. A soulful prayer is bound to influence the whole world. Prayer is to be truthful and humble. It has bearings on One's relationship with his fellowbeings. For Gandhiji, prayer is the key of the morning and the evening. He said, "Begin your day with prayer and make it so soulful that it may remain with you until the evening. Close the day with prayer so that you may have a peaceful night free from dreams and nightmares. Do not worry about the form of prayer. Let it be any form, it should be such as can put us into communion with the divine. Only, whatever be the form, let not the spirit wander while the words of prayer run on out of your mouth."[6]

Gandhiji laid great stress on daily prayer. Regarding the type of prayer, he said that the freshness does not consist in the variety of *bhajans* or other recitations but should result from the increasing purity of our heart. We should grow daily more contended and feel greater peace of mind. If we do not have this experience, the fault will lie not with the quality of the prayers but with the element of untruthfulness in us. Prayer is offered with confidence with the hope that God is approachable.

Gandhiji believes in the philosophy of Karma and Rebirth. To him, the law of Karma is inexorable and impossible of evasion. There is thus hardly any need for God to interfere. We are the makers of our own destiny. We can mend or mar the present and on that will depend the future. Regarding Rebirth, he said, "I believe in rebirth as much as I believe in the existence of my present body. I, therefore, know that even a little effort is not wasted."[7] The acceptance of the law of Karma, however, does not mean to Gandhiji, that our life and activities are completely determined. Such determination paralyses moral effort and cuts at the very root of ethics.

The doctrine of Karma does not contradict the free will. The free will we enjoy is less than that of a passenger on a crowded deck, because our previous Karmas limit the range for the exercise of our free will. But, the little freedom that we have is real in the sense that we are free to choose how we use that freedom. Gandhiji does not believe in complete freedom. Such freedom will mean chaos.

Gandhiji was a social reformer who preached everything for the benefit of the human society. To him, religion has got practical importance in life. He tried to spiritualise all aspects of human life. His concept of religion is wide, tolerant and comprehensive. The application of the scientific methods to the field of religion strikes at the very root of the meaning and significance of religion. Religion is the basic need of a man. It is instinctive and impulsive. It has rooted in our nature and is as old as weeping or smiling.

Gandhiji was one of the personalities of India who believed that religion is a creative force in life. He was very much to develop the ethical basis of religion. To him, religion must necessarily be pragmatic. A multi-religious society struggling for socio-political progress needs an all embracing conception of religion which can bind people of divergent faiths together for a joint march towards a new social reconstruction. He does not believe that religious affairs can be kept divorced from political affairs. He said that religion which takes no account of practical affairs and does not help to solve them, is no religion. Religion, for him, is a living faith which derives sustenance from devotion to a spiritual being which is most fully revealed to us as Truth. He believes that religion is always subject to a process of evolution and re-interpretation. Progress towards truth, towards God, is possible only because of such evolution.

Gandhiji did not accept traditional or conventional religion. He did not adhere to any religious principle uncritically. He was influenced by the eastern and western religious thinkers. He dedicated his life to the service of the masses, which was the essence of his religion. Religion is the basis on which all life structure has to be erected, if life is to be complete. No man can live without religion.

Gandhiji was deeply religious. Without religion, life for him was not worth living. He used the term 'religion' in a wider sense. He held that religion was a term of wide connotation. He inherited his religious forum from his parents. His family background shaped his religious thoughts to a certain extent. His parents observed periodic fasts. He said, "In Rajkot, however I got an early grounding in toleration for all branches of

Hinduism and sister religions. For my father and mother would visit the Haveli as also Shiva's and Rama's temples, and would take or send us (youngsters) there. Jain monks also would pay frequent visits to my father. . . . They would talk with my father on subjects - religious and mundane. Besides he had Musalman and Parsi friends, who would talk to him about their own faiths, and he would listen to them always with respect, and often with interest. Being his nurse, I often had a change to be present at these talks. These many things combined to inculcate in me a toleration, for all faiths".[8]

To quote P.F. Power, "Other religious philosophies touched him during his childhood, but especially Jainism. This is a reform group external to orthodox Hinduism and composed mainly of urban trading classes. Jains search for ultimate truth beyond the senses and take a vow of non-injury to avoid harm to all living things, including micro-organisms. This pledge of personal non-violence is *ahimsa,* found also in Buddhism and Hinduism as a virtue of the man who renounces the world. Under different influences Gandhiji later interpreted and expanded this principle to include temporal and collective as well as spiritual and individual matters."[9]

Manusmriti moulded Gandhiji's religious thought. He said, "But the fact that I had learnt to be tolerant to other religions did not mean that I had any living faith in God. I about this time to come across *Manusmriti* which was amongst my father's collection. The story of the creation and similar things did not impress me very much, but on the contrary made me incline somewhat towards athesism. But one thing took deep root in me — the conviction that morality is the basis of things, and that truth is the substance of all morality. Truth became my sole objective. It began to grow in magnitude every day, my definition of it also has been ever widening."[10]

Gandhiji was very much influenced by Buddhism. *The Light of Asia* influenced him. He said, "The brothers also recommended the *Light of Asia* by Sir Edwin Arnold, whom I know till then as the author only of the song Celestial, and I read it with even greater interest that I did the *Bhagvadgita*. Once I had begun it I could not leave off."[11]

Gita also influenced Gandhiji. Renunciation in action is the message of the *Gita.* It is a book of spiritual reference to him. He said, "But after forty years unremitting endeavour fully to enforce the teaching of the *Gita* in my own life, I have in all humility, felt that perfect renunciation is impossible without perfect observance of ahimsa in every shape and form."[12] The *Gita* inspires us to do our duties, neglecting the suffering and the torture that we receive in course of our action. He said that he who gives up action falls. He who gives up only the reward rises. But renunciation of fruit in no way means indifference to the result. In regard to every action, one must know the result that is expected to follow, the means thereto, and the capacity for it. He, who, being thus equipped, is without desire for the result and is yet wholly engrossed in the due fulfilment of the task before him is said to have renounced the fruits of his action.

Gandhiji's deep interest and devotion to Christianity made him realise its importance. "The Sermon on the Mount" especially created an indelible impression on his mind. He said, "I have not been able to see any difference between the Sermon on the Mount and the *Bhagvadgita.* What the Sermon describes in a graphic manner, the *Bhagvadgita* reduces to a scientific formula. It may not be a scientific book in the accepted sense of term, but it has argued out the law of love — the law of abandon as I call it - in a scientific manner. The Sermon on the Mount gives the same law in the wonderful language. Today, supposing, I was deprived of the *Gita* and forget all its contents but had a copy of the Sermon, I should derive the same joy from it as I do from the *Gita.*"[13] The major religions of the world influenced him and shaped his course of life.

By religion, Gandhiji does not mean formal religion, or customary religion, but that religion which underlies all religions, which brings us face to face with our Maker. Religion should pervade every one of our actions. Here religion does not mean sectaranism. It means a belief in ordered moral government of the universe. It is not less real because it is unseen. This religion transcends Hinduism, Islam, Christianity, etc. It does not supersede them. It harmonises them and gives them reality. He said, "Let me explain what I mean by religion. It is not the Hindu religion which I certainly prize above all other religions, but the religion which transcends Hinduism, which changes one's very nature, which binds one indissolubly to the truth within and which ever purifies. It is the permanent element in human nature which counts no cost too great in order to find full expression and which leaves the soul utterly restless until it has found itself, known its Maker and appreciated the true correspondence between the Maker and itself."[14]

Gandhiji remarked that no man can live without religion. There are some, who, in the egotism of their reason declare that they have nothing to do with religion. But it is like a man saying that he breathes but that he has no nose. Whether by reason, or by instinct, or by superstition, man acknowledges some sort of relationship with the divine. The rankest agnostic or athesist does acknowledge the need of a moral principle and associates something good with its observance and something but with its non-observance. Bradleaugh, whose athesism is well known, always insisted on proclaiming his innermost conviction. He had to suffer a lot for thus speaking the truth, but he delighted in it and said that truth is its own reward. Not that he was quite insensible to the joy resulting from the observance of truth. This joy however is not all worldly, but springs out of communion with the divine. That is why he said that even a man who disowns religion cannot and does not live without religion.

To quote Gandhiji, "My Hindu instinct tells me that all religions are more or less true. All proceed from the same God, but all are imperfect because they have come down to through imperfect human instrumentality."[15] Religions are different road converging to the same point. What does it matter that we take different roads, so long as we reach the same goal? In reality, there are as many religions as there are individuals. In theory, since there is one God, there can be only one religion. But in practice, no two persons have had the same identical conception of God. Therefore, there will, perhaps, always be different religions answering to, different temperaments and climatic conditions, he said.

Gandhiji's basic motive was purely religious and he could not lead a religious life unless he identified himself with the whole of mankind and he could not do that without participating in politics. He considered religion more important than his country and that he was thus a Hindu first and a nationalist second. Politics is the application of religion to him. His ideas were based upon religious tradition, not political, jurisdical, philosophical or economic. He always tried to base his political and economic doctrine on religion. His political and economic ideas are to be found in religious tradition. The fact that Gandhiji was a religious reformer means that he had clear, or at least working criteria for right belief. Religion was not for him simply a devout feeling or respect for holy things. On countless occasions, he attacked the exploitation and senselessness which occur in the name of religion.

When Gandhiji speaks of religion, he does not mean any conventional or usual religion, but that religion which is at the root of all religions and that this fundamental religion harmonises the historical religions and makes them valid. Just as a tree has one trunk but many branches and leaves, so there is one true and perfect religion, although it is divided into many, as it appears through a human intermediary. He briefly defines religion as a trust in the moral organisation of the universe. The goal of man's life is to conquer evil in himself and reach the good.

Religions are different roads to the same goal. For this, one must not reject other religions, but anybody belonging to any religion can receive from others what is good in them. He considered religion to be a very personal matter. It is based upon the individual's own experience and ability to understand. He considers it the duty of every civilised man and women to read with sympathy the writings of every religion.

Gandhiji's religion may be characterised as ethical spiritualism. To him, any religion without a moral foundation ceased to be a religion. Religion and morality were two faces of the same coin wherein neither of them could be separated from each other. He held the view that religion was to morality what water was to the seed sown in the soil. He found the essence of religion in morality or ethics. Morals, ethics and religion are convertible terms. A moral life without reference to religion is like a house built upon sand. And religion divorced from morality is like 'sounding brass' goods only for making a noise and breaking heads.

Gandhiji interpreted religion with the day-to-day problems. His mission was not only to humanise religion but also to moralise it. His ultimate aim in equating religion with morality was to make religion dynamically operative in human life. He was quite sure that the biggest challenge to religions was not from the side of 'atheists' but rituals and dogmatists. To him, scriptures cannot transcend reason and truth. They are intended to purify reason and illuminate truth. He rejected all religious doctrine that does not appeal to reasons. He says that error can claim no exemption even if it can be supported by the scriptures of the world.

Gandhiji preached consistently about the power of truth and *ahimsa* based on the equality of all human beings, the regulations of human desires, the purity of means and ends, and simplicity of life. He had a dynamic concept of religion with its essence to be found in morality and truth. He believed in the fundamental value of all religions which emphasised the absolute value of truth, morality and justice.

Gandhiji said that there could not be any politics without religion and that he entered politics because he was primarily a religious man. He said, "But though by disclaiming Sainthood, I disappoint the critics expectations, I would have him give up his regrets by answering him that the politicians in me has never dominated a single decision of mine, and if I seek to take part in politics, it is only because politics encircle us today like the coil of a snake from which one cannot get out, no matter how much one tries. I wish, therefore, to wrestle with the snake, as I have been doing with more or less success consciously since 1894, unconsciously, as I have now discovered, ever since, reaching years of discretion. Quite selfishly, as I wish to live in peace in the midst of a bellowing storm howling round me, I have been experimenting with myself and friends by introducing religion into politics".[16] He believed that a religious individual could overcome the savage instinct in man and substituting in its place human capacity for good and noble deeds. He introduced religion into politics by identifying himself with service to humanity. He remarked that politics bereft of religion are absolute dirt ever to be shunned. Politics concern nations and that which concern the welfare of nations must be one of the concerns of a man who is religiously inclined.

Gandhiji believed that even in the political sphere religion has a special role to play. He was of the opinion that the religious men were politicians in disguise. He held the view that ethical values like humanity, forgiveness, tolerance, etc., which were intrinsic to every religion were good antidote to the arrogance of power-hungry politicians. He said, "For me the road to salvation lies through incessant toil in the service of my country and the humanity. I want to identify myself with everything that lives. In the language of the *Gita*, I want to live at peace with both friend and foe. So my patriotism is, for me, a stage on my journey to the land of eternal freedom and peace. Thus, it will be seen that for me there are no politics devoid of religion. They subserve religion. Politics bereft of religion are a death-trap because they kill the soul."[17]

Gandhiji felt that a religious motive was in tune with an individual's desire to take part in politics. There was no question of dividing social, political and religious dimensions into watertight compartments. He took an enlightened view of religion whose objective was to popularise progressive social, political and economic ideas. To him, any religion that gave sanction to antiquate and repressive social custom and tyrannical political authority was the negation of true religion.

Gandhiji considered all castes and communities as equal. He was secular in the sense that he was against coercion to seek conformity to certain creeds. He did not believe in state religion even though the whole community had one religion. He was against the state aid to religious bodies. He distinguished between religion and ethics. He regarded religion as a private matter but the teachings of ethics were certainly a major concern of the state.

Gandhiji's religion is not the religion of merely uttering the name of God. To him, religion is not pride, pedantry or sophistry. He did not mean this or that religion, a denominational faith, or a creed or a sect. His religion is the science of soul and God. He held that religion means recognising the self, recognition of the cosmic life, recognition of reality, seeing God face to face, attaining *Moksha* through service to man.

II

Some sociologists have arrived at the conclusion that the idea of God is a creation of the unscientific terro-stricken mind of the primitive man. They hold that as the light of science will spread, this darkness present in the form of belief in God will also disappear. Had God really been darkness, His disappearence would both have been necessary and beneficial. The God of those is surely in danger who have conceived Him as different from the soul, as the creator of the universe and as one who resides in some corner outside the world in the seventh or forty-ninth heaven. But such is not the conception of God taught by the Vedanta. The Supreme is the purest form of soul and devotion to God is the acme of self-efforts. Vinoba believes that God exists. If all our earthly body, etc., was taken away, there would still be something left, a consciousness, which is supremely us. There is that something in everyone. And just as our body is a world, so at the same time we are all parts of a greater world and all our consciousness are parts of a mighty whole. That is God. God means truth and love. Where these two come together, God manifests Himself. Truth, love and compassion, these have been regarded to be the forms of God.

Mystics are able to see God with their eyes. Men of God all over the world testify to this fact. Universal brotherhood will not be established in the world unless the paternal authority of God is accepted. If anyone believes in the goodness of man, Vinoba will be satisfied. Belief in human goodness is the beginning of belief in God. Therefore, if one believes in the essential goodness of man, he will be on the right path. This will naturally deepen his experience and he may reach the stage of realising God.

An atheist is he who does not believe that good actions produce good results and bad actions, bad results. Atheist is one who believes in the theory of *Karma*, even though he has no faith in God. None becomes religious by invoking the name of religion, and nor does he become a devotee by taking the name of God. One who lacks integrity in life, non-violence in conduct, religiousness in dealings, cannot be atheist. A sincere atheist is nearer to God than a nominal theist. More atheism has been spread by conflicts among theist than by atheists themselves. Atheism is not a new phenomenon. It is as old as faith in God. There is no room to hold that atheism is more prevalent these days.

Exploitation of our fellow-men means disrespect to God. If we harbour pride and consider ourselves in some way superior to others, that too implies disrespect to God. Devotion must express itself in our day-to-day life. Compassion, love and sympathy are the outer expressions of devotion. A person who has real devotion will see the image of God that resides in every human heart. The highest way of devotion is surely shedding all narrow personal self-interest. The one characteristic of the devotee is that he reduces himself to Zero and believes that whatever exists around him is the manifestation of God who is perfect. The devotee shall always bear in mind that all men and women who live around him are so many forms of his Master and he is their servant. This is true service, true surrender as the servant to the Master, and indeed this is true devotion. Vinoba, however, warned that if one who has devoted himself to the service of all around him begins to feel that he was doing something big, something particularly meritorious, and so begins to cultivate pride within himself that he is superior to his fellows on that account, then surely his service of his fellow-men will not be devotion.

God is truth, all good, fearless and devoid of animosity. If we worship God but do not develop His qualities, we should consider our worship to have been in vain. The form of worship of God has changed. Those who would not realise it, would be doing wrong things in the name of devotion. We continue to worship with flowers and fruits but without genuine devotion. God is to be sought in our hearts. He can be worshipped only with flowers of real devotion and the fruits of an incessant quest of true knowledge.

God has innumerable attributes. A devotee worships Him as one endowed with the particular quality he finds himself lacking in. Different religions differ from each other since they have developed in different regions. However, they all aim at worshipping God. He has innumerable forms, and may even be said to be formless. Of these innumerable forms, some prefer one and some prefer others. This variety in worship removes the monotony of life. Just as several melodies go to make music complete, similarly the various forms of worship make the devotion complete.

Prayer is an effort of a living being to remember God gratefully. In spite of the fact that the various religions, all built up by the services and sacrifices of many great men, have some major or minor differences in their doctrines and observations, there is no difference of opinion in any religion on this matter that prayer performed collectively or individually, by repetitions of His name or in some other way, is indispensable both for the individual as well as society, for his or its life, moral uplift, purification of mind, search for truth and maintenance of mental equilibrium in the sorrows and attachments of life.

Prayer is the last act of our daily routine. During working hours we do many acts of commissions and omissions. At the end of the day, we stand before Him and say: Merciful and Ominiscient Lord! Thou knowest everything, even without our expressing them in so many words. But we feel a consolation in speaking about Thee in our language. So we pray, let us not take credit and feel proud of—whatever good acts we have performed. Save us from pride and give us the wisdom to do acts without egotism. We might also have committed wrongs, some knowingly and others unknowingly. Forgive us all these failings. By forgiveness we do not mean that we should escape from the punishments for such acts. Do punish us, for thy punishment itself is forgiveness. But have favour on us and guard us against committing such sins. If we open our hearts before Him in this way, we would experience as if a wondrous beam of light entered our heart and illuminated and strengthened our being. There is no source of energy in the world which, if we draw from it, does not decrease, except the one emanating from God, who is within us.

Vinoba compares prayer to a bath, food and sleep. It has the virtues of all the three. Sleep gives rest and replenishes energy. Prayer also provides rest and imparts spiritual strength to man. While food nourishes the physical body, prayer does the same to the mind and heart. A bath cleanses this body, while the prayer purifies the mind and heart. Thus what all these three do together for the physical body, prayer does for the mind and heart. Through doing his duty, man tries to clean his mind and heart.

Prayer is no mechanical activity. It is not simply performed by words of mouth. It involves the practice of passing the whole day in the light of the spirit of the words of the prayer, impressing one's heart with it. All of us describe God reverently in our own ways but it has not been said that a particular description is His best or complete description. God is still satisfied with it just as a father is satisfied with the inarticulate expressions of his tiny child. Even so, silent prayer is accepted as one of the best forms of prayer. If children and parents sit together in silent prayer, it is a good practice and elevates society. The habit of silence will be conducive to peace and non-violence. Silence expresses the feeling for God more than words ever can. Everyone can contemplate on the God of his conception when he is silent. It is only in silence that one can experience God in the recesses of one's heart. In silence, one's intellect is submerged in the feeling for God. Both individual and collective prayer have utility in their respective fields. Collective prayer is necessary for social consciousness. Unison of voice strengthens the feeling of unity. At the same time, individual prayer should not be given up.

Man is not simply an animal. The predominating quality of an animal is vitality, *prana.* It is not so with man. The word *manusya*, man, stands for one who contemplates, who thinks. In the case of animals their capacity is limited. But it is not so with man. Man differs from an animal in that he is not satisfied merely with meeting the demands of the body. There is the urge in him to get rid of social bonds and to identify himself with the whole world. This is the thirst of the soul. In case the two are satisfied together, there would be peace and amity in society. God has bestowed three gifts on man — speech, organs of actions and a sympathetic heart. A man can measure his development by the extent he has been able to control his mind and heart and his mind has calmed down. The original state of the soul is that of calmness. Hence real progress will be presumed to lie in the attainment of the utmost tranquillity.

A man has both good and evil desires, but, on the whole, it is the good desires that prove more powerful and it is they which bring him satisfaction. A man's heart, we must understand, is always good at the core. It may get rusted outside due to various external factors; its internal goodness remains always the same, whatever the outward appearance. By nature, man is noble. That is why he pays respect to righteous persons and not to thieves and dacoits. Man is forced to act wrongly by the force of circumstances. He is carried away by the currents. But the moment he would realise it, he would change at once on one plea or another. One good point about those who are really wicked is that they have great faith in God. They are quite near to those who are really virtuous, like the two ends of a circle. That makes their conversion quite easy. People might have become devoid of morality, but they have not acquired love for immorality. They love truth and morality. The present lust for money is due to the existing economic structure being based on it. If the social order be such that people get work and their needs are satisfied, selfish people will be turned into good people.

The supreme ideal of a man's life is *Mukti*, liberation. The attainment of happiness is not the purpose of life, for it is a quality of the soul itself. None can survive without joy, no matter whether there is less or more of it. The real purpose is self-realisation. Liberation consists in ridding oneself in the larger self of the society. *Moksha* is liberation from attachment, anger, lust, illusion, ignorance, etc. If these perversions have been got rid of, *Moksha* has been attained.

The fulfilment of being born as a human being does not lie in the enjoyment of physical pleasures, but in making others happy, no matter how little it be. A life full of service is 'life'. The rest of it is only a form of death. But if the service is not selfless, it does not remain service. Happiness does not mean the pleasure of the heart or mind. Pleasure has little to do with happiness. Happiness is abiding, pleasure is transient. Many people today are suffering mentally and emotionally for the sake of their country. They find happiness in such suffering. This is because suffering is sometimes salutary, as it is when accompanied by a sense of benignent service. True happiness is to be found in peace, not in a disturbed or agitated consciousness. Its source is tranquillity of spirit. We feel happy only when we are overpowered by the feeling of oneness.

Desire, anger and greed are the three great enemies of an aspirant. Greed is the most universal and subtle among them. In reality, the enemy is not outside but inside. Our indolence, desire for indulgence, mutual quarrels, ego preventing unity between us, ignorance, these are the enemies, and they appear externally assuming the form of outsiders. Hence our first task is to destroy the inner enemies, and then the external ones would disappear without efforts. A righteous man does not die. As long as he is alive, he is confined to only one physical body. But when he dies, he does not remain imprisioned in one body . If a godly man leaves the body and he has no desire left, he lives in the world through many bodies, and it is what is termed liberation.

An important idea in Hinduism is that of rebirth. According to it, if a person is not able to complete the work he is doing in any particular birth, he tries to complete it in the next. Thus he goes on evolving. After once being born as a humen being, one would, latter on, either get human birth or some higher one. However, if some desire of his is so strong that it could only be satisfied as an animal, he would get that birth and would even relish it. It is a mistake to think that one is born rich or poor in accordance with his deeds in the previous birth being good or bad. Good deeds of the past birth result in good thoughts and freedom from egotism, while evil actions give rise to evil desires and to proclivity for wrong deeds. An individual soul has its own regular chain of *sanskaras,* tendencies, and he is born of particular parents accordingly. His own regular chain constitutes one line and a second one is constituted of family tendencies. The individual soul is born at the point of their intersection.

We shall certainly reap in the next birth the consequences of the actions of the present one. But some good and bad deeds are so intense that their fruits are experienced in this very life. The Indian people have some wrong conceptions. They think that pleasures and pains experienced by us are the fruits of actions of the previous births. Hence everyone must put up with one's fate. This is a mistaken idea. No doubt, everyone has his own destiny. Yet, some part of it is common. We are born in the same village because of it. Thus what comes to be destined does not pertain to an individual alone. The law of *Karma* is not to penalise you. The award of punishment is an indication of God's love. He wishes to reform you. There is something over and above justice, and it is Mercy. We must reap the consequences of our evil, deeds, but if God takes mercy on us, we can be exempted from them. No matter how wicked one is, if he is repetant he becomes a good man.

Man has enough freedom to carve out his future. He has been given a free hand to decide what he would like to become in his next birth. God will not impose His will on us in this matter. If you want to continue whirling in the cycle of life and death, He will ordain it. Or if you want to move closer to God with the hope of merging in Him one day, it is also possible. We get the physical body in accordance with the previous birth, but as soon as we have been born, the effects of our previous life are over. After that it depends on ourselves how we would act. This would determine our next birth. What is termed as 'fate' are the efforts of yesterday and the efforts of today would determine the fate of tomorrow.

The word *dharma* is comprehensive. The ethics which sustains our life is called dharma. Dharma deals with several matters—soul and God, worldiy life and the life hereafter, the rules of conduct in this world. All these form its subject matter.

A religion deals with several matters. One is 'worship' involving direct relationship with God, the second is 'ethics' concerned with truth, non-violence, etc. The third are 'customs' and 'practices' which pertain to various rites performed at death, birth etc. The fourth is mythology, stories, etc. Thus a religion has several components. The more we concentrate on the fundamental oneness of humanity, the more do the different religions appears as enriching and strengthening one another. Vinoba regards the different religions as merely different forms of worship. Each form has its distinctive merit. When the different ways meet together all these merits gather together and make a rich and full pattern. The ethical principles are the same in all religions. All religions lead to God. They are like different roads; one seems to go to the east, another to the west, but still everyone leading to and terminating in God.

Organisation and religion are contradiction in terms. Due to organisation, religion has not become that force it would otherwise have become. Surely, the progress would have been slow, yet the condition would have been far better than what it is today. There are many who pride in the name of religion, there are many who start trouble in the name of religion, but there are few who practice the essence of religion. Religion and love must flow freely within a society. We like to keep our God in a distant heaven. We are afraid to bring Him down to the earth.

The subject matters of science and religion are different. The situation is similar to that of eyes and ears between whom there is no opposition because they have their independent fields. Some hold that science is opposed to religion. They feel that religion would die because of science. But, Vinoba thinks otherwise. Upto now there was no science and consequently, really speaking, religion had not come into existence. Now as science would advance, pure religion would survive and not the false one. Only a religion which is rational, which is not a figment of imagination, which has arisen above desires and has done away with all sorts of distinctions including that of worship, would be able to survive.

Karmayoga does not mean becoming less spiritual in attitude. It would not only result in fruits equal to those of *Dhyanayoga* but in something more. In the path of action one is expected to utilise to the maximum this earthly sheath — this physical body with all its powers — for promoting good. All the organs of work and the senses of perception including the mind and the intellect, etc., have to be employed methodically with a view to purifying them in course of time. Action is as fuel to knowledge. In order to keep the sacrificial fire of knowledge constantly burning, one must supply the fuel in the form of action. The essence of the matter is that the *Karmayogi*, by surrendering the desire for fruit, receives an infinite reward. This society in which he moves is happy. He attains inward purity and also *jnana*. And society being rid of hypocrisy and deceit, the ideal of a perfect life comes within our reach. This, experience shows, is the greatness of a *Karmayogi*.

Both the *sannayasi* and *karmayogi* are *jnanis*, seers, and are entitled to the same high throne. Though the names are different, the substance is the same. They are two modes of the same reality. A wheel in rapid motion seems at rest. The state of the *sanayasi* is similar. From his *shanti*, his peace and steadiness, flows infinite power, endless movement. Though all the endeavours of the *sanayasi* have ceased, and come to a rest, he does mighty deeds. To do nothing, and yet to do all things, is possible for the *siddha*, the perfected one, not for the *sadhak*, the seeker. *Karmayoga* is both the way and the goal, but *sanyas* is only goal. From the point of view of the *sadhak*, *Karmayoga* is preferable to *sanyasa*.

One should utter the name of God, use one's hands in doing God's work and see Him inside his own self. When all these three go on together, the path of devotion is accomplished in all its aspects. In the path of devotion, remembering the name of God has been glorified. *Nirguna* and *saguna* complement each other, they are not incompatible. Starting from *saguna*, one has to tread the path to the goal of *nirguna; nirguna* too needs the water of saguna to cleanse the subtle impurities of the mind. Each gains lustre from the other.

There are three important things in *dhyanayoga* (the *yoga* of meditation), namely: (1) one-pointedness of mind; (2) setting bound to one's life, to help to achieve this; and (3) a state of equanimity or evenness of vision. One-pointedness of mind means controlling its movements. Setting bound to one's life means doing actions after weighing and measuring them. Evenness of vision means having the nobility to think in terms of the whole world. These three together make up *dhyanayoga*. To achieve these three, one needs the help of practice and detachment.

Spirituality is that science which enables you to perceive and recognise the whole infinite universe in your own self. It is impossible to comprehend fully the true nature of the universe and to find out who is its creator, for the universe is macrocosmic as well as microcosmic. And yet an effort can be made to comprehend its nature. This effort can be made through observation which could be either outward or inward. Physics helps to understand the outward aspects of the universe, while metaphysics enables us to comprehend a little the inner nature of the universe. It is, however, not possible to attain to integral knowledge through the pursuit of physical sciences. To try to know who is the Creator and to realise Him is again more difficult. That is why the only easy way of knowing and realising Him is to try to find Him in the individual self. This itself is known as spirituality.

It is wrong to separate spiritual progress and material advance. If the two are conceived separately, both will remain incomplete. It cannot be said that materially backward countries are spiritually advanced, while it is equally fallacious to think that materially developed countries like America are spiritually poor. Where there is only apparent material abundance, decay will be discernible; and where the emphasis is one-sidedly on spiritual progress, there too life will be lopsided. Thus progress can only be all-sided.

REFERENCES

1. *Young India*, 5-3-25.
2. M.K. Gandhi, *In Search of the Supreme*, Vol.I, p.6.
3. *Gandhi Marg*, Feb.1983, p.620.
4. M.K. Gandhi, *Hindu Dharma*, p.67.
5. M.K. Gandhi, *Prayer*, p.171.
6. M.K. Gandhi, *In Search of the Supreme*, Vol.I, p.176.
7. *Young India*, Vol. II, p.1204.
8. M.K. Gandhi, *My Experiments with Truth*, p.449.
9. P.F. Power, *Gandhi on World Affairs*, p.10.
10. M.K. Gandhi, *My Experiments With Truth*, pp.50-51.
11. *Ibid*, p.91.
12. *Ibid*, p.215.
13. M.K. Gandhi, *Christian Mission, their Place in India*, p.123.
14. *Young India*, 12-5-20.
15. *Ibid.*, 29.5.24.
16. *Ibid.*, 12-5-20.
17. *Ibid.*, 3-4-24.

3

ETHICAL THOUGHT OF GANDHI AND VINOBA

Gandhi had asserted that morality should be the ultimate authority in the conduct of human affairs, in the sphere of economics, politics, society etc. Moralisation of politics had been the dream of many political thinkers; to make it a reality had been the endeavour of Gandhiji. He was one of the greatest moralists. He applied his moral force for the society. His morality consists of purity of soul and motive, nobleness of character, selfless service and the goodness of means. He tried to solve all the problems on the basis of morality. He laid much stress on spirituality. His spirituality was nothing else but what he considered to be universal morality.

To Gandhiji, religion is to morality what water is to the seed that is sown in the soil. True religion and true morality are inseparably bound up with each other. Morality is the essence of religion. Religion is synonymous with allegiance to the moral law. He would reject any religious doctrine that does not appeal to reason and is in conflict with morality. To him, religion and morality are identical. He saw that while religions might differ widely in their theologies, they were strikingly alike in their moral teachings. Morality stresses the relation of the individual to society and religion stresses the relation of individual to God. He held that morality is binding upon us, because it is the eternal and immutable law of nature. It is its own reward. The moral law is independent of our feelings and opinions, but it has its seat in the soul of every man. Truth is within ourselves.

While explaining Gandhiji's standard of moral life, J.B. Kripalani said, "Gandhiji lives a simple life, a life of self-discipline and restraint. His wants are few. His joys are natural and innocent. But it must not be forgotten that simplicity is itself the middle path. It is moderation, avoiding the two extremes of over-indulgence of the senses and the suppression. Simplicity consists in the regulation of one's desires. But in an age which has made pleasure, sensation, and continual excitement as the be-all and end-all of life, it is no wonder that Gandhiji's simplicity should be considered as ascetic. In an age in which the highest worship is of a Mammon, Gandhiji's giving up wealth and its pursuit for a noble cause may be considered as an act of great renunciation. In an age which looks upon the artificial stimulation of wants and their multiplication as the sign of culture and civilisation, Gandhiji's limitation of his physical requirements to those that are necessary for a healthy and vigorous life may pass for mortification of the flesh. But in no healthy normal society can his life be considered as one of mortification of the flesh".[1] Morality is a means of realising the truth. We cannot reach truth without morality.

Gandhian morality centres round the philosophy of *Gita*. All actions are to be dictated by God. To him, *Gita* was composed in the background of *himsa*. But the ultimate teaching of *Gita* is *ahimsa*. Action to be moral must be voluntary. The actions of men are neither moral nor immoral at sometimes. He said that the question of morality does not enter at all into many of our ordinary actions. Since we are, for the most part, the mere creatures of convention. Morality arises in a problematic situation only to decide the correct thing. This does not arise if there is lack of intention to do good to others. Morality is not innate in man. But it is the quality to be acquired. Gandhiji's concept of morality breaks with conservatism. He said that true morality consists not in following the beaten track, but in finding out the true path for ourselves and in fearlessly following it.

Morality is what man ought to do. Morality consists in the right or the good behaviour of men. Gandhiji advocated flexibility between the behaviour of an individual and that of mankind as a whole. He did not accept virtue as obedience to customs. His approach to morality is practical, for he did not stress, what a moral act is. His idea of morality is governed by two principles — one is the idea of superiority in respect of quality, and the other is internal sanction. He did not stress much on the former. Actions which come out from heart and are performed out of true moral sense form the morality. The real seat of morality is contained in the nature of man himself. To him, morality is neither one's imagination nor a timeless service. He said, "If any action of mine claimed to be spiritual is proved to be unpractical it must be pronounced to be a failure. I do believe that the most spiritual act is the most practical in the true sense of the term".[2]

To Gandhiji, morality must be universal in nature. He said that the highest moral law is that we should unremittingly work for the good of mankind. His morality lay in the common good. He did not believe in mere utilitarian formula of 'the greatest good of the greatest number'. So long as man remains selfish and does not care for the happiness of others, he is no better than an animal and perhaps worse. His superiority to the animal is seen only when we find him caring for his family. He is still more human, that is, much higher than the animal, when he extends his concept of the family to include his country or community as well. He climbs still higher in the scale when he comes to regard the human race as his family, said Gandhiji. He was in favour of prescribing a common norm for all men. He was opposed to relative morality. He stressed the need for universal morality.

Gandhiji took truth and non-violence as the universal principles of morality and he considered them as absolute. For moralising the conduct of man, he prescribed the 'Vows'. To him, morality is the very foundation of life. The existence and progress of man depends upon his moral self.

Gandhiji drafted a code of rules (vows) — democratically after consulting all the inmates who readily consented and kept them all. This demonstrated their strength and enabled them to overcome the manifold temptations of daily life. Realising the human feelings, he observed that the taking of a vow does not mean that we are able to observe it completely from the very beginning, it does mean constant and honest effort in thought, word and deed with a view to the fulfilment. A vow means inflinching determination, and helps us against temptations. The meaning of vow is commitment to an injunction voluntarily imposed on oneself, as a means to an end which is worthy to be chosen. A vow is not any kind of commitment, but one with a clear ethico-religious significance. There cannot be a vow to commit sin; in the case of a vow, first thought should be clear, if, later it is found to be sinful, then arises the necessity to give it up. But no one takes, or ought to take vows about dubious matters. Vows can be taken only on points of universally recognised principles. A vow once taken cannot be broken. Taking vows is not a sign of weakness but of strength. Gandhiji is convinced of the supreme necessity of vows for the purpose of self-purification and self-realisation. The vow which he prescribes for the ashramites may appear difficult to practise. But once practised, their lives would be simple and in tune with nature. To him, a life without vows is like a ship without anchor or like an edifice that is built on slip sand instead of a solid rock. A vow imparts stability, ballast and firmness to one's character.

Truth, for Gandhiji was the first and foremost as he identified it, with God. It was not merely a policy but in thought and action as well. Even for the sake of anything, one should not practise deception in any form. One must be prepared to undergo any suffering for the sake of truth. He conceded that what appeared as truth to one person might not do so to another. The entire philosophy of *satyagraha* is based on the fact that truth alone can be victorious, for truth is 'that which is', while untruth means 'non-existent'. Truth can be distinguished into Relative Truth and Absolute Truth. To attain Absolute Truth, we should hold by the Relative Truth. There is no religion higher than truth. He considered truth as God. He said that where there is truth, there also is knowledge which is true, where there is no truth, there can be no true knowledge. That is why the word *Cit* is associated with the name of God. And where there is true knowledge, there is always bliss. There sorrow has no place. And even as truth is eternal so is the bliss derived from it. Hence we know God, *Sat-Cit-Ananda.* One who combines in Himself truth, knowledge and bliss. Truth without non-violence is not truth but untruth. In his opinion, constant endeavour, indifference to other interests of life and the vows of truth, non-violence, *brahmacharya*, non-stealing, non-possession, etc., are indispensable for the realisation of truth.

Ahimsa literally means non-killing but Gandhiji broadened its meaning by adding an important positive element. The followers of *ahimsa* were bound not only to hurt any living things, but also to love everybody. He took pains to distinguish it from injustice which can never be tolerated but protested non-violently. To him, *ahimsa* is the heart of all religions. The means and the end are one, so *ahimsa* is truth itself, its very soul. Truth and *ahimsa* are like the two sides of a smooth unstamped metallic disc and are so intertwined that it is difficult to disentangle and separate them. Truth is the highest law, but *ahimsa* is the highest duty. The path of *ahimsa* is as narrow as it is straight, even like the path of truth. It is like balancing oneself on the edge of a sword. By concentration, an acrobat can walk on a rope. But the concentration required to tread the path of truth and *ahimsa* is far greater. The slighest inattention brings one tottering to the ground. One can realise truth and *ahimsa* only by ceaseless striving. The principle of *ahimsa* is hurt by every evil thought, by undue haste, by lying, by hatred, by wishing ill to anybody. It is also violated by one's holding on to what the world needs. Gandhiji did not regard non-violence simply as avoidance of physical injury to animate beings. His non-violence aimed at liberating men and women from inner as well as outer violence. *Ahimsa* means avoiding injury to anything on earth in thought, word or deed.

Brahmacharya is the foundation for other vows. Generally *brahmacharya* means control over sex. Eytomologically it means the discipline which leads to the realistion of Brahman. Gandhiji defines *brahmacharya* as 'that correct way which leads to Brahman'. It did not mean mere control of sexual passion, it meant control of all the organs of the sense. One who attempts to control only one sense and allows the others to be free is 'bound to end in failure'. To hear suggestive stories, to see suggestive sights, to taste stimulating food or to touch exciting things and at the same time to try to control the only remaining stimulus, was to Gandhiji, like putting one's hand in the fire and expecting to take it out unhurt. He rejects the traditional belief that women being morally inferior to men and that one seeking to attain *brahmacharya* should avoid contact with them. It is not woman whose touch defiles man, but he is himself often too impure to touch her. He does not mean that only unmarried people could observe *brahmacharya*. Even if a person is married he can observe this vow if he establishes with his wife a relationship based on purity and friendship and not on lust. He conceded that there were difficulties involved in practising self-control and continence in the light of his own experience. He felt that absolute continence was the ideal worth feeling, but he did not consider physical union between married couples as violation of *brahmacharya* so long as such union was purely for the sake of progeny. He admitted that it would not have been possible for him to be a pure *satyagrahi* without the vow of *brahmacharya*.

Control of the palate is the outcome of many of Gandhiji's dietic experiments for keeping the vow of *brahmacharya*. This vow cannot be practised in isolation from the other vows. He said, "Control of the palate is very closely connected with the observance of *brahmacharya*. I have found from experience that the observance of celibacy becomes very easy, if one acquires mastery over the palate. This does not figure among the observances of time-honoured recognition.... We of the *satyagraha ashram* have elevated it to the ranks of an independent observance and must therefore consider it by itself".[3] He firmly believed that food is taken essentially for sustenance and not for pleasure or to satisfy the palate. He also knew well that it was difficult to master the palate. Food has to be taken like medicine. The body is injured by over-eating which can partially be repaired only by fasting. 'His motto was everyone should eat to live and not live to eat'. He conducted experiments in controlling taste and found them to be completely successful. *Asvada* means that we should be extremely simple in our food, eating not to please our palate but to keep the body in proper working condition. The *vrata* of *asvada* calls for continual mindfulness. The body is to be nourished with a view to keeping it as a fit instrument for service. The votary of truth has to realise the perfect conquest of the palate depends on His grace. *Asvada* is a part of the foundations of the good life which clearly involves control of all the senses.

Non-stealing is a vow to be followed by anybody persuing vows of truth and non-violence. But to Gandhiji this vow is more than just that. Not only taking another and appropriating something in the belief that it is nobody's property, but also receiving something which one does not need, a father eating something secretly, keeping his children in the dark, improper multiplication of one's wants, coveting anybody's belongings, bothering about things to be acquired in the future, plagiarism, etc. —all these are instances of physical or mental offences against the vow of non-stealing. Need based requirements for immediate use when obtained through legitimate process ensured fulfilment of this vow. He pointed out that man succumbs to accumulation of articles not needed immediately due to uncertainities of future and greed. He did not like the persistence of worldly desires in his wife. He considered it unlawful for her to keep money received as a gift from other persons; for him it constituted an act of theft. He was very strict in regard to practice of honesty in day-to-day matters. Non-stealing calls for the effort to abstain from conditions which bar the manifestation of truth. But *asteya* is related to both truth and *ahimsa*. Non-stealing wants us to face the truth of our basic needs.

Non-possession vow becomes a logical extension of vow of non-stealing. Non-possession and non-stealing do not necessarily lead to economic want. Gandhiji says that riches remain, we only change our attitude to them. He analysed man's need and placed them in order of value. A follower of truth could not hold anything for tomorrow. Limitations of wants could only promote real happiness and contentment. He held that if each retained possession only of what he needed for a simple living, no one would be in want and all would live in contentment. Civilisation in the real sense of the term consists not in the multiplication but in the deliberate and voluntary reduction of wants. Non-possession means non-dependence of material things. It implies total abolition of private property in all kinds of belongings, a view more radical that of extreme communities. Absolute non-possession is an abstraction and is unattainable in its fulness. *Aparigraha* is non-possession. Possession implies provision for the future. He tries to extend non-possession to the spiritual field. 'He who fills his brain with useless knowledge violates this principle of action. He who steals an idea from another and presents it as his own is guilty of stealing ideas'. *Aparigraha* is not confined to conduct and property but Gandhiji relates to it 'thoughts as well'.

Fearlessness is indispensable for the growth of truth and non-violence. Gandhiji considered fear to be so evil that he rather advised violence than cowardice and submission, if there were no other alternatives. Truth and non-violence can be cultivated only by the strong and strength lies in absence of fear, not in the quality of flesh and muscle we may have on our bodies. Fearlessness means freedom from all external fear — fear of disease, bodily injury and death, of dispossession, of losing one's nearest and dearest, of losing reputation or giving offence and so on. A seeker after truth must conquer all these fears. He should be ready to sacrifice all in the quest of truth even as Harichandra did. Gandhiji lays stress on the need of prayer and of unflinching obedience to dictates of conscience, for the voice of conscience is the will of God and final judge of the rightness of every deed and every thought. He suggested to derive strength from God who alone has to be feared for he believed that when we fear God, we shall fear no man, low or high placed he may be. He emphasised the need of cultivating self-confidence as a necessary part of the practice of fearlessness. Truth and fearlessness are closely linked with each other. We have to be fearless if we want to ascertain, face, uphold, elicit, and suffer for truth.

Bread labour comes next. Gandhiji believed that to live, man must work. He derives the principle of bread labour from reading Tolstoy's writings. He said that God created man to work for his food and those who eat without work were thieves. Bread labour is a corollary of the principle of non-stealing and a means of realising non-possession. He feels that if people were convinced of the value and necessity of bread labour, there never would be any want of bread, cloth. Spinning deserves to become the universal form of bread labour. He said that a *satyagrahi* occupies himself in productive work. There is no easier and better productive work for millions than spinning. No other village craft has the capacity that spinning and its auxiliary processes have for putting so much money into the pockets of the largest number of villagers with minimum of capital outlay and organisational effort. Bread labour does not include intellectual labour. Those who earn more than necessary for their requirement must use the bulk of their greater earnings for the good of the community. Non-possession and bread labour would lead to economic equality. Gandhiji said, "My ideal is equal distribution, but so far as I can see, it cannot be realised. I therefore, work for equitable distribution".[4] He advocated work as the only solution to eradicate the poverty.

Swadeshi is closely related to truth and non-violence. It means belonging to or made in one's own country. Gandhiji defined *swadeshi* as the spirit in us which restricts us to the use and service of our immediate surroundings to the exclusion of the more remote. In the field of economics, a *satyagrahi* must use only things that are produced by his immediate neighbours and serve those industries by making them efficient and complete where they might be found wanting. Gandhiji stands for the self-sufficiency of the country and even of villages except for such foreign things as are needed for the growth of the people. To him, the broad definition of *swadeshi* is the use of all home-made articles to the exclusion of foreign things, in so far as such use is necessary for the protection of home industries, more specially those industries without which India will become pauperized. To reject foreign manufacturers merely because they are foreign and to go on wasting national time and money in the promotion of one's country of manufacturers for which it is not suited would be criminal foly, and a negation of the *swadeshi* spirit. He said that it is the greatest delusion to suppose that the duty of the *swadeshi* begins and ends with merely spinning some yarn anyhow and wearing *khadi* made from it. *Khadi* is the first indispensable step. A votary of *swadeshi* will carefully study his environment and try to help his neighbours wherever possible, by giving preference to local manufacturers even if they are of an inferior grade of dearer in price than things manufactured elsewhere. *Swadeshi* stands for duty and pure service.

Untouchability stands for the idea that a man is polluted if he touches someone who is born in a so-called low family or does some menial work. The removal of untouchability vow follows from the principle of spiritual unity of all life. Gandhiji maintained untouchability as the sin of the Hindus. He believed in *varna* system. He hoped that *swaraj* was a meaningless term if about forty million people were kept under perpetual subjection and deliberately denied the fruits of national culture. The law of *varna* rules out untouchability. The *ashram* did not believe in sub-castes. Nevertheless the *ashram* believed that *varnas* and *ashramas* were essential elements of Hinduism. The purpose of every work is the same. All are born to serve God's creation. Gandhiji refuses to restrict untouchability to the suppressed classes and wants us to love all life as our own selves and serve the whole world. He wanted every Indian to take a vow to work for the removal of untouchability. It is a great tragedy that functional classification of the society has degenerated into caste-classification where in mutual respect has given place to hostility and frequent atrocities are committed on helpless people who are engaged in inferior activity. Constitutional and legal provisions also seems to be fanning the 'wind of hatred'.

Toleration of all religions is the last vow. Gandhiji believes in the equality of the principal religions of the world. He prefers to call it as equality of all religions to tolerance of all religions. To him, the different religions are beautiful flowers from the same garden or branches of the same majestic tree. He held all religions were equally true, though being received and interpreted through human instruments equally imperfect. He was not in favour of conversion from one religion to another. He felt that all religions were equally glorious and that those who were born Hindus need not search for truth in other religions. A *satyagrahi* should honour and study all religions. The study will help him to grasp the basic unity of all religions and to cultivate equimindedness towards them. Equal respect for religions does not mean toleration of irreligion or being blind to the faults of other faiths. No single religion can claim to be perfect. He said that everybody is right from his own point, but it is not impossible that everybody is wrong. In each religion, we could see the same fundamental morality. We have to respect the basic teachings of all religious faiths equally, but to give due value to each other's religion of sentiments. The seekers of truth should have an equal vision of all religions. If we follow the law of love, we shall not bear any hatred towards the irreligious brother. Gandhiji not only enjoins equality of respect for all religions, but pleads for the incorporation of the good features of other faiths into one's own.

II

A law of *dharma*, morality, to be true must be applicable to all. Any such rule which is applicable to some and not to others, is no *dharma* at all. To speak truth, to love all mankind, to be compassionate, all these rules are applicable to all. Vinoba does not differentiate between moral and spiritual planes. Spiritual plane is higher, but the moral plane is not lower. It is nearer humanity. One is the ladder, the other, the destination. It is not possible for a man to be a spiritual being without first being a moral being. It is our duty to act in a manner conducive to a proper functioning of the creation, society and the physical body. We build up many good or bad institutions, but these three are no creation of ours. Hence it is our inherent duty to make good the harm done to these three institutions through *yajna, dana* and *tapa*. A right action is one that gives us peace of mind; an unrighteous action is that which deprives us of it.

Svadharma implies that every person has his own independent duties. It vary from individual to individual. But since a man is also a part of society, we may say that everyone should render service to society. However, each has his own special qualities and he should serve society by developing them well. The *svadharma* of the *Gita* is so comprehensive that it is applicable to all. To determine one's *svadharma*, one should consider what is helpful and appropriate to one's nature and situation, and what duty falls to one. Different individuals may have different *svadharma*. The *svadharma* of an individual may also vary from time to time. The *dharma* of an individual person varies according to the times and the development of his inclinations. The *Gita* teaches that the *svadharma* of an individual consists of his duties at a particular time. When a man is born, his *svadharma* too is born with him.

The number of the observances can be less or more and it does not vary, but non-violence, truth and some others are eternal. The vows have the capacity of protecting men and society. As a result of their observance, an individual like Gandhiji became a *mahatma*. They embody the quintessence of the lives of all saints. They are not only meant for a recluse. They are for him and for the whole society. It is said these days that 'vows' constitute a bondage, but it is a misleading idea. The vows do not give trouble. They form a good straight path. When the road is good, we do not worry. Vows imply treading a straight path. They make it easy, they make men free.

The world is sustained by truth. It subsists because there is more truth in the world than untruth. If untruth acquires predominance over truth, the world would come to an end. There is no inherent strength in untruth. Even for its existence , it has necessarily to depend upon truth. Four means have been suggested for the realisation of self. The first among them is truth, and it is very important. If we put all the moral philosophy of the world on one side and truth on the other, the latter would outweigh. Truth is the highest principle of morality, while all others are secondary to it. Truth is that which makes us realise the existence of conscience and brings satisfaction to it. When the conscience does not feel satisfied or is shocked, there is untruth. That is, the conscience is witness to truth and untruth. Truth cannot be defined. It is self-evident. As a mater of fact man is essentially truthful by nature. Truth is more natural than untruth. We see this in children. Gandhiji said that truth could be attained by non-violence. Vinoba's idea is that truth can be attained by humility, objectivity and non-insistence. It is so in science. There is no dogmatism in it. Only that is considered as correct which is testified by experiment. Truth and beauty are not opposed to each other.

Non-violence does not mean 'not to commit violence'. Its one meaning is to be fearless, the second is to cooperate lovingly, and the third is to have faith in constructive work. It is not merely an external activity. It is an inner faith. It is the name for the maintenance of balance in thinking and not allowing the equanimity of mind to be disturbed. It is that which keeps different persons together and which tries to seek non-difference in differences, while violence is that which creates divisions and increase differences. A life of non-violence means not merely occasional sacrifice but perpetual sacrifice, but joy in sacrifice. Non-attachment and universal love are necessary if we wish to practise non-violence. The strength of non-violence lies in the balance in thinkings, gentleness in words and restraint in actions. Impatience does not help in the growth of non-violence. There is no dearth of weapons in the armoury of non-violence. It can never fail. Non-violence has such capacity that even if the whole world is drowning, a single individual can save himself by swimming. The power of non-violence does not depend upon number, but on inner purity. There is no conflict between non-violence and legislation. A non-violent movement prepares the minds of the people, and if a legislation is enacted in accordance with it, it comes within non-violence. The characteristic of non-violence is that everyone has full freedom and yet every one follows voluntarily all rules and regulations. Non-violence needs discipline and planning much more than violence. It does not mean lenient tolerance; not does it mean intolerable vigorous restraint.

Brahmacharya means that a man directs the path of his life to the search for Brahman. It is a positive concept. It does not merely means that we have to avoid any particular thing, but there is something tangible, positive, to be done. It means the greatest aim of all, achieving the realisation of the lord. In *brahmacharya* it is important to lead the senses and the mind into the right direction. If we think in terms of suppressing them, our evolution will be hindered. Therefore, all the senses should be rightly used. They should be correctly restrained; this will be very helpful to aspirants. As long as the vow of *brahmacharya* is not observed, the observance of the vows of truth and non-violence is well-nigh impossible. The reading of sacred books, and the company of saintly men, is certainly a great help towards a life of *brahmacharya.* But to live a natural life in the open air, and to work bare bodied in the sunlight, is an even greater help. It is a wrong idea that a *brahmachari* should avoid coming in contact with women. It leads to the imposition of unnecessary artificial restrictions. If a *brahmachari* feels that he should not look at any women who may have come before him, we should regard that as his shortcoming. *Brahmacharya* imparts greater acuteness to intelligence. Today, world population is increasing rapidly and the available land is decreasing. Therefore, people are saying that we should have small families. This means that *brahmacharya* now has a new social context.

The observance of *brahmacharya* is found difficult because we are not able to control our palate. An important measure of success in that spiritual endeavour is the degree of victory over palate. That is why control of the palate is reckoned as a vow, and in accordance with it, an aspirant should take care that his diet becomes purer and cleaner. Food is only a means to maintain the physical body. It should not be accorded greater importance. If we are slave to the palate, we consume more than we need. This makes society suffer. One fond of tasty food is a slave and he undermines his strength. If we overeat, our sexual passion is excited. Consequently, we do harm to society. For true service, purity in food is necessary. As is the food so is the mind. The food we eat should be regulated. Not what food we take, but how much we take, is the more important question. It does matter what food we choose to eat, but it matters even more that it is in right measure.

Non-stealing does not merely mean taking a thing not given by others, but also accepting something without giving anything to others. Consumption without sacrifice is theft. It is theft to use foodgrains, cloth and other things without directly participating in their production.

Non-possession is a name for 'liberality', though people understand it differently. They hold that non-possession stands for poverty. But it is not so. In fact it means that no sooner there is accumulation, it is to be passed on to another. Where wealth flows, it is non-possession. The true meaning of *aparigraha* is to discard the sense of identity with one's body. For, the body itself is the main thing among one's accumulation. There is no external measurement for non-possession. Vinoba holds that one may even be observing it though living in great splendour. Hence there can be no external measurement. Let everyone find answer within himself. When a man deals in the world, he comes to acquire possessions, however less. Hence the way to be free of that sin is to surrender a part of it to society. When non-possession comes to be recognised as the basic principle of social order, there will be minimum need of power to coerce for the government to rule. There are five features of a non-possessive society, namely,

(i) there will be an abundance of wealth;
(ii) the wealth will be equally distributed among the members of the society;
(iii) there will be no accumulation of such rubbish as liquor and cigarettes;
(iv) there will be accumulation of certain things on priority basis, the order being foodgrains, cloth, housing, agricultural implements, means of knowledge, means of recreation and so on; and
(v) there will be minimum accumulation of money.

The vow of non-stealing regulates the mode of acquiring wealth, while the vow of non-possession regulates the quantity. In consequence, both are one and the same. Non-stealing and non-possession supplement each other in making economic dealings moral, without which *dharma* cannot be established in individual and social life. Truth and non-violence are basic, but in the economic field they can only find expression in non-stealing and non-possession. Economic matters play a very big role in life and the science of morality cannot be indifferent to it. On the contrary, it is the responsibility of ethics to regulate and control it. In the *shastras,* non-possession is considered as a necessary concomitant of non-stealing. If theft is regarded as a crime, accumulation of property and inequality also must be regarded as sinful, whereas at present one is punished and the other is praised.

Bread labour should be done as a worship. It should be a daily rule with us not to take food without doing some physical labour. Vinoba will not give food to anyone, be he even a professor or a judge, unless he has worked for two to four hours. Non-violence cannot be attained without physical labour. Today bodily labour commands no prestige in society. The peasant works hard but he likes to see his son on some job in an office. Bread labour alone is a mode prescribed by nature for man to earn his living. An observance of this vow makes the observance of others easy. If one gets bored by physical labour, it is a sign of degeneration. The *varna* system does not mean that some should be absolutely exempt from physical labour. It only means that everyone should contribute his share to the society in accordance with his capacities. It is wrong to say that some may do only physical labour while others do only mental labour. God has created us with brains, hands and also hunger. If he had desired that only a few persons should produce things and others should do only intellectual work, He would have given only brains to some and only hands to others, for He is omnipotent. But he has not done so. He has given hunger to all and so also hands. It is, therefore, against his will that some persons do only intellectual work like reading, writing, etc., and the rest merely do the physical labour of production.

Fearlessness represents a state of mind which can be brought about only by a change in the way of man's thinking. It can only be derived from the inner self. If one has the inner strength to die rather than to live with indignity, a child even can face any danger fearlessly. Fear and morality are mutually contradictory. A disposition to fearlessness is the basis of divine virtues. If one leads a virtuous life in constant fear of temptations, death would lose its dreadfulness. Fearlessness is of three kinds — fearlessness based on knowledge, fearlessness based on God and fearlessness based on discernment. Fearlessness based on knowledge is that fearlessness which results from the knowledge of dangers and the irremedies. The fearlessness based on God, makes one fully fearless. But it cannot be acquired without prolonged efforts, devotion and continued practice. Fearlessness based on discernment restraints one from needless and reckless darings, and if one has no option but to face a danger, it makes him do so keeping his mind calm out of discernment.

Swadeshi means self-reliance in a comprehensive sense. It is an inherent duty of man. Just as non-violence is an established rule of *dharma*, similarly *swadeshi* is a rule of conduct. Things nearer to us, be it the neighbours, prevailing customs or morality, are inherited by us, and therefore, are dear to us. In this lies the secret of *swadeshi*. If we boycott articles giving an extreme interpretation to the moral duty of *swadeshi,* we shall prove ourselves to be men of a long past world. We shall be antiquated. It is not that *swadeshi* forbids dealings with outsiders. There is good scope in it for reciprocal dealings. But it is wrong to burden others with work we can well do ourselves. In short, the plan should be one which will make each village a self-sufficient unit with regard to food, cloth, education etc.

The idea of having equal feelings for all religions also implies the acknowledgment that one's own religion is imperfect. If we are imperfect, the religions conceived by us are also imperfect. All religions are partial embodiments of truth. The various religions should be understood as different forms of worship. Vinoba was of the opinion that there are four essential ingredients of *sarva-dharma-sambhava,* the feeling of equality for all religions. One of them is faith in one's own religion; the second is respect for all religions; the third is the reformation of one's religion; and the fourth one, which naturally follows from the three, is opposition to irreligiousness. When all these four ingredients are found together, there is *sarva-dharma-sambhava.*

The task of eradicating untouchability has got to be done in two ways: (1) by improving the economic condition and mentality of the *Harijans*; and (2) by purifying the Hindu religion. Vinoba coined the word *sparsha-bhavana* (the feeling of touchability). This word is comprehensive. The feeling should be that we should have touch with the whole world.

In addition to the above eleven vows, Vinoba introduced one more vow, namely, *Anida* which means not to speak ill of others. We should only talk of the good qualities of a man in his absence. If we have to point out his shortcomings, it should be done to him in private or in the presence of friends before whom it would not be improper to do so. If we hear something praiseworthy about someone, we should be inclined to agree with it immediately. If we hear something evil, our heart and mind should not be prone to accept it. We should not look upon anybody with suspicion. It acts as a great obstacle in the way of devotion and service.

REFERENCES

1. Viswanath Tandon, *The Social and Political Philosophy of Sarvodaya After Gandhi,* Sarva Seva Sangh Prakashan, Varanasi, 1965, p.199.
2. N.K. Bose, *Selections From Gandhi,* Navajeevan Publishing House, Ahmedabad, 1957, p.255.
3. M.K. Gandhi, *From Yeravada Mandir*, pp. 24-29.
4. *Young India,* Vol. II, p.124.

4

SOCIAL THOUGHT OF GANDHI AND VINOBA

Gandhiji has made some contribution in the social field. Throughout his life, he advocated to establish a classless and stateless society. His social philosophy aims at the attainment of both material and spiritual prosperities. There should not be any differentiation of caste, creed, colour and sex in such a society. The present society is the modification of the past society. Man has lived in society from the very beginning. Man cannot live without society. In every society, the individuals should get equal opportunities and facilities for their development. Gandhiji wanted to establish a new society which is free from exploitation and oppression. He pained to see the chaotic conditions of the society. He aimed at a society based on love, peace and non-violence.

Between individual and society, the individual comes first in Gandhiji's philosophy, though society is by no means neglected. Society must provide opportunities for the maximum growth of the individual which consists in selfless service of society and willing fulfilment of his social obligations. The difference between individual and society disappears in *sarvodaya*. Individual is considered as a unit of society and society is considered as a group of individuals. Man is a live principle and society is dynamic. Man is the nucleus of the entire society, and the society is organic whole.

Gandhiji regards *Varnashrama dharma* as Hinduism's unique gift to the world. To him, it is a law of our being which, no matter howsoever much we may deny, cannot be abrogated. It is a universal law, like the law of gravitation and equally inexorable. It governs the entire human family. He said that *varna* means predetermination of the choice of man's profession. The law of *varna* is that a man shall follow the profession of his ancestors for earning his livelihood. Every child naturally follows the colour of his father, or chooses his father's profession. *Varna*, therefore, is in a way of law of heredity. *Varna* is not a thing that is superimposed on Hindus, but men who were trustees for their welfare discovered the law for them. It is not a human invention, but an immutable law of nature — the statement of a tendency that is ever present and at work like Newton's law of gravitation. Just as law of gravitation existed even before it was discovered, so did the law of *varna*. It was given to the Hindus to discover that law. By their discovery and application of certain laws of nature, the peoples of the West have easily increased their material possessions. Similarly, Hindus by their discovery of this irresistable social tendency have been able to achieve in the spiritual field what no other nation in the world has achieved.

The law of *varna* defines man's mission on this earth as to know his Maker. For the realisation and fulfilment of this mission, it is imperative that man must not devote the chief part of his life, to making experiments in finding out what occupation will best suit him for earning his livelihood. On the contrary, Gandhiji will recognise that it is best for him to follow his father's occupation, and devote his spare time and talent to qualifying himself for the taste to which mankind is called.

Varnasharma is not a system of watertight compartments. It is a recognition to one of a scientific fact, whether we know it or not. A *Brahmin* is not only a teacher, he is predominantly that. But a *Brahmin* who refuses to labour will be voted down as an idiot. The *Rishis* who lived in the forests, cut and fetched wood, tended cattle and even fought. But their pursuit in life was pre-eminently search after truth. Similarly, a *Rajput* without learning was good for nothing, no matter how will he wielded the sword. And a *Vaishya*, without divine knowledge sufficient for his own growth, will be a veritable monster eating into the vitals or society as many modern Vaishyas, whether of the East or the West have become. According to *Gita*, they are incarnations of sin who live only for themselves.

Regarding untouchability and caste, Gandhiji said, "I draw a sharp distinction between untouchability and *varna* or caste. The former has no scientific basis. It cannot be supported by reason. It denies man the privilege of service to fellow-beings and deprives the untouchables in distress of the right of receiving service from their kind. The caste system has, in my opinion, a scientific basis. Reason does not revolt against it. If it has disadvantages, it has also its advantages. It does not prevent a *Brahmin* from serving his *Shudra* brother. Caste creates a social and moral restraint. The doctrine of caste cannot be extended. I would restrict it to four divisions. Any multiplication would be an evil. I would reform the castes and rid them of undoubted abuses, but I can find no reason for their abolition. For me, there is no question of superiority or inferiority. *Brahmin,* who regards himself as a superior being born to look down upon the other castes, is not a *Brahmin.* If he is first, he is so by right of service".[1]

Gandhiji remarked, "But I do regard *varnashrama* as a healthy division of work based on birth. The present ideas of caste are a perversion of the original. There is no question with me of superiority or inferiority. It is purely a question of duty. I have indeed stated that *varna* is based on birth. But I have also said that it is possible for a *Shudra,* for instance to become a *Vaishya.* . . . He who performs the duty of a *Brahmin* will easily become one in the next incarnation".[2]

Varnashrama dharma is a universal law stated in so many words by Hinduism. It is a law of spiritual economics. Nations of the west and Islàm itself unwillingly are obliged to follow that law. It has nothing to do with superiority or inferiority. The customs about eating, drinking and marriage are no integral part of *varnashrama dharma.* It was a law discovered by your anscestors and my ancestors, the *Rishis* who saw that if they were to give the best part of their lives to God and to the world, and not to themselves, they must recognise that it is the law of heredity. It is a law designed to set free man's energy for higher pursuits to life. . . . My *varnashrama* enables me to dine with anybody who will give me clean food, be he Hindu, Muslim, Christian, Parsi whatevér he is, my *varnashrama* accommodates *Panchama* families with whom I dine with the greatest pleasure, to dine with whom is a privilege. My *varnashrama* refuses to bow the head before the greatest potentate on earth, but my *varnashrama* compels me to bow down my head in all humility before knowledge, before purity, before every person, where I see God face to face, said Gandhiji.

To quote Gandhiji, *"Varnashrama dharma* is humility. Whilst I have said that all men and women are born equal, I do not wish, therefore, to suggest that qualities are not inherited; but on the contrary, I believe that just as everyone inherits a particular form, so does he inherits the particular characteristics and qualities of his progenitors, and to make the admission is to conserve one's energy. That frank admission, if he will act upto it, would put a legitimate curb upon our material ambitions, and thereby our energy is set free for extending the field of spiritual research and spiritual evolution. It is this doctrine of *varnashrama dharma* which I have always accepted".[3]

Gandhiji said, *"Ashrama* is a necessary corollary to what I have stated to you; and if *varna* to-day has become distorted, *ashrama* has altogether disappeared. *Ashrama* means the four stages in one's life. The *Brahmachari*, at least up to 25 years, are entitled to enter upon the second *Ashrama*, i.e., the *grihastha*. And because the whole conception of Hinduism is to make man better than he is and draw him nearer to his Maker, the *Rishis* set a limit even to the *Grihastha ashrama* stage and imposed on us the obligation of *vanaprastha* or *sanyasi*. But today you will vainly search throughout the length and breadth of India for a true *brahmachari,* for a true *Grihastha,* not to talk of a *vanaprastha* and *sanyasi.* We may, in our elongated wisdom laugh at this scheme of life. But I have no doubt whatsover that this is the secret of the great success of Hinduism. The Hindu civilisation has survived the Egyptian, the Asyrian and the Babylonian. The Christian is but two thousand years old. The Islamic is but of yesterday. Great as both these are, they are in my humble opinion, in the making. Christian Europe is not at all Christian, but is grouping for its great secret; and there is today a competition, healthy as also extremely unhealthy and ugly, between these three great religions".[4]

Varna and *ashrama* are two different words. The institution of four *ashramas* enables one the better to fulfil the purpose of life for which the law of *varna* is necessary. Gandhiji remarked, "So far as I am aware, the *ashrama* arrangement is unknown outside India; but even in India, it has practically disappeared at present. There is no such thing now as *brahmacharya*, which is intended to be the foundation of life. For the rest, we have *sanyasis*, most of them such only in name with nothing of *sanyasa* about them except the orange robe. Many of them are ignorant, and some who have acquired learning are not knowers of *Brahma* but fanatics. There are some honourable exceptions, but even these well conducted monks lack the lustre we love to associate with *sanyasa.* It is possible that some real *sanyasis* lead a solitary life. But it is obvious that *sanyasa,* as a stage in life, has fallen into destitute. A society which is served by able *sanyasis* would not be poor in spirit, unprovided even with the necessities of life, and politically dependent, as Hindu society is at present. If *sanyasa* were with us a living thing, it would exert a powerful influence on neighbouring faiths, for the *sanyasi* is a servant not only of Hinduism but all of the faiths of mankind. But we can never hope to see such *sanyasis* unless *brahmacharya* is observed in the country. As for *vanaprastha*, there is no trace of it. The last stage we have to consider is that of the house-holder. But our house-holders are given to unregulated self-indulgence. House-holders, in the absence of the other *ashramas,* live like brutes. Self-restraint is the only thing which differentiates man from beast, but it is practised no longer".[5]

Gandhiji remarked that if the *ashrama* scheme has broken down, the plight of the *varnas* is equally bad. At first there were four classes; but now there are innumerable sections or only one. If we take it that there are as many *varnas* as there are castes and sub-castes, their name is legion, on the other hand, if as I think *varna* have nothing to do with caste, there is only a single *varna* left and that is the *shudra*. We are there not finding fault with anybody but only stating the facts of the case. *Shudras* are those who serve and are dependent upon others. India is a dependency; therefore, every Indian is a *shudra*. The cultivator does not own his land, the merchant his merchandise. There is hardly a *Kshatriya* or a *Brahmin* who possesses the virtues which the *shastras* attribute to his *varna*.

Gandhiji said, "*Varnashrama*, as I interpret it, satisfies the religious, social and economic needs of a community. It satisfies the religious needs because a whole community accepting the law is free to devote ample time to spiritual perfection. Observance of the law obviates social evils and entirely prevents the killing economic competition. And if it is regarded as a law laying down, not the rights or the privileges of the community governed by it, but their duties, it ensures the fairest possible distribution of wealth, though it may not be an ideal, i.e. strictly equal distribution. Therefore, when people in . . . it leads to confusion of *varna* and ultimate disruption of society. In this law, there is question of compelling any person to follow the parental occupation against his or her aptitude, that is to say, there can be no compulsion from without as there was none for, perhaps, several thousand years, during which the law of *varnashrama* worked without interruption. By training, the people had recognised the duty and the justice of the law, and they voluntarily lived under it. Today, nations are living in ignorance and breach of that law and they are suffering for it. The so-called civilised nations have by no means reached a state which they can at all regard with equanimity and satisfaction".[6]

According to *Shastras*, Brahmins are expected to spend themselves in the service of religion by *tapas*, social service and the quest of Brahma or Truth. It is a pity that modern Brahmin not only pay them and do not serve religion, but follow all manner of professions to enrich themselves. A true Brahmin should be the very image of humility and not be proud of his knowledge or wisdom. A Brahmin would cease to be a Brahmin if he considers himself superior to others, as it is his duty to teach people to look upon a Brahmin and a *Bhangi* with an equal eye. Again, a Brahmin is hardly worth the name, if he does not have the courage of his own convictions. We must fear the Lord and none else. Cowardice is incompatible with divine wisdom, said Gandhiji.

Varna today has become a means of arrogating to oneself a higher status. The real *varna* of Gandhiji's conception does not exist today. In the purest type of Hinduism, a Brahmin, an ant, an elephant and a dog-eater are of the same status. And because our philosophy is so high, and we have failed to live up to it, that every philosophy today stinks in our nostrils. Hinduism insists on the brotherhood not only of all mankind, but of all that lives. It is a conception which makes one giddy, but we have to work upto it. The moment we have restored real living equality between man and man, we shall be able to establish equality between man and the whole creation. When that day comes, we shall have peace on earth and goodwill to men.

To quote Gandhiji, "Caste has nothing to do with religion. It is a custom whose origin I do not know and do not need to know for the satisfaction of my spiritual hunger. But I do know that it is harmful both to spiritual and national growth. *Varna* and *ashrama* are institutions which have nothing to do with castes. The law of *varna* teaches us that we have each one of us to earn our bread by following the ancestral calling. It defines not our rights, but our duties. It necessarily has reference to callings that are conducive to the welfare of humanity, and to no other. It also follows that there is no calling too low and none too high. All are good, lawful, and absolutely equal in status. The callings of a Brahmin — spiritual teacher and a scavenger are equal, and their due performance carries equal merit before God, and at one time seems to have carried identical regard before man. Both were entitled to their livelihood and no more. Indeed, one traces even now in the villages the faint lines of this healthy operation of the law. Living in Surgeon *(Sevagram)* with its population of 600. . . . I do not find a great disparity between the earnings of different tradesmen, including Brahmins. I find, too, that real Brahmins are to be found even in those degenerate days, who are living on alms freely given to them and are giving freely of what they have of spiritual treasures. It would be wrong and improper to judge the law of *varna* by its caricature in the lives of men who profess to belong to a *varna*, whilst they openly commit a breach of its only operative rule. Arrogation of a superior status by any of the *varnas* over another, is denial of the law. And there is nothing in the law of *varna* to warrant a belief in untouchability. I am aware that my interpretation of Hinduism will be disputed by many. . . . That does not affect my position. It is an interpretation by which I have lived for nearly half a century, and according to which I have endeavoured to the best of my ability to regulate my life."[7]

Gandhiji remarked, "As I have made it clear over and over again, there is no real *varna* today. When we have come to our own, when we have cleansed ourselves, we may have the four *varnas* according to the way in which we can express the best in us. But *varna* then will invest no one with a superior status or right, it will invest one with higher responsibility and duties. Those who will impart knowledge in a spirit of service, will be called Brahmins. They will assume no superior airs, but will be true servants of society. When inequality of status or right is ended, everyone of us will be equal. I do not know, however, when we shall be able to revive true *varna dharma.* Its real revival would mean true democracy".[8]

Women have suffered gross social and economic injustices at the hands of the community. Gandhiji exposed the cause of women with great concern. He had advocated the abolition of all economic and legal disabilities from which women in India suffer today. He is opposed to the suppression of women, whether by law or by custom. He had almost dramatically, in an unprecedented manner, brought our women to the forefront and converted them into an important functional group of our population. If today women in India are enjoying so many facilities, particularly some equality with men, it is because of the sudden and spectacular call from Gandhiji to join his world-renowned political struggle for freedom for India. He had seriously taken up the unfinished task of the early reformers and began to work earnestly for its completion.

Gandhiji wants mutual consultation and cooperation between men and women. Men have considered themselves to be lords and masters of women instead of considering them as their friends and co-workers. Women is not a competitor of man, nor an inferior or weaker sex, but only a complementary to her male partner. The art of bringing up the infants of the races is women's special and sole prerogative. Without her care the races must become extinct. Man and woman are a peerless pair being supplementary to one another, each helps the growth of other, and without the support of one the other cannot conceive. To him, women is economical and careful, never rash, maintains balance and conserves what is good and pure. Both men and women are fundamentally one, but in the form there is difference. He held that it is the man who earns the bread and the woman who distributes the bread. Women is the company of man, gifted with equal mental capacities. She has the right to participate in the capacities of man and she has an equal right of freedom and liberty comparatively. It is incorrect to call women as weaker sex.

Gandhiji did not differentiate between man and woman. He wants woman to take part in social and political activities. They should not consider themselves inferior to man. He advises woman to resort to civil rebellion against all undesirable and unworthy restraints. On the other hand, man should learn to give place to woman. Woman is the personification of self-sacrifice. Women endures several sufferings during child-birth and child-rearing. She suffers daily so that her baby may wax from day to day. Let her transfer that love to the whole of humanity. He advised the women to reawaken the old spirit of self-sacrifice, love and inner strength in themselves. We will have to produce women, pure, firm and self controlled, as Sita, Damayanti and Draupadi. If we produce them, such modern sisters will receive the same homage from Hindu society as is being paid to their prototypes of yore. He wanted women to be at least aware of their position and the actual hardships that they had been undergoing.

A woman should be given equal opportunity and privilege to serve the society. A women is apt to social work, nursing, education, etc. In Gandhiji's opinion, it is degrading for man and woman that she should be called upon or induced to foresake the hearth and shoulder the rifle for the protection of the hearth. It is a reversion to barbarity from beginning to end. In 1918, he said that women is the companion of man gifted with equal mental capacities. She has the right to participate in every minutest detail in the actitivites of man, she has an equal right of freedom. She is entitled to a supreme place in her own spheres of activity, as man is in his.

Gandhiji maintained that the ideal of marriage is more spiritual than physical. The purpose of marriage is not self-indulgence, but self-control. It is not to the body that one is married. In marriage two souls come together not to seek bodily pleasure but to strive for their own growth and refinement. When the body of one partner disappears the union becomes all the closer. One of the wishes, expressed by the husband during the marriage ceremony is that the bride may be the mother of good and healthy sons. This does not mean that procreation is obligatory but means that if progeny is wanted, marriage performed in a strictly religious spirit is essential. He who does not want a child need not marry at all. Marriage for the satisfaction of sexual appetite is no marriage.

The creation of a new life is nearest to the divine and one should approach that act in a divine way. Man and woman must come together with no other desire than that of creating a new life. Man forgets that he is nearest to the divine, hankers after the brute instinct in himself and becomes less than the brute. The right education in our country is to teach woman the art of saying 'no' even to her husband, to teach her that no part of her body to become a mere tool or doll in her husband's hand. The first thing is to free her from mental slavery, to teach her the sacredness of her body and to teach her the dignity of national service and the service of humanity.

Gandhiji believed that divorce should be granted within well-defined limits. A husband cannot demand obedience from his wife, through his right obtained by marriage. *Purdah* system was not common in the country. He says that the *purdah* in India is a recent institution and was adopted during the period of Hindu decline. In the age when proud Draupadi and spotless Sita lived, there could be no *purdah*. Gargi could not have held her discourses from behind the *purdah*. All the education that we have been receiving from the past hundred years seems to have produced but little impression upon us, that the *purdah* is being retained even in educated households, not because the educated men believe in it themselves, but because they will not manfully resist the brutal custom and sweep it away at a stroke.

Gandhiji was against child marraige. The custom of child marriage is both a moral as well as a physical evil for it undermines our morals and induces physical degeneration. When people suggested legislation to raise the age consent to eradicate the obnoxious custom, Gandhiji had said that it might be good for bringing a minority to book, but then it is not legislation that will cure a popular evil. It is an enlightened public opinion that can do it. He said that a father has no right to arrange early marriage of his children.

Gandhiji was against the dowry system. He encouraged inter-caste marriages. He advised the women of India to remain unmarried rather than be a party to a marriage arranged on the basis of dowry. He remarked, there is no doubt that the custom is heartless. But so far as I am aware it does not touch the millions. The custom is confined to the middle class who are a drop in the ocean of Indian humanity. These, however, does not mean that one may ignore the dowry evil because it is confined to a comparatively small number of people of the country. The system has to go. Marriage must cease to be a matter of arrangement made by parents for money. The system is intimately connected with caste. So long as the choice is restricted to a few hundred young men, or women in a particular caste, the system will persist no matter what is said against it. The girls or boys or their parents will have to break the bonds of caste if the evil has to be eradicated. Then, the age for marrying has also to be raised and the girls have to dare to remain spinsters, if need be, if they do not get a suitable match. All this means, education of a character that will revolutionize the mentality of the nation. Unfortunately, the system of education has no connection with our surroundings which therefore remain practically untouched.

Gandhiji was against enforced widowhood, while glorifying the grace of voluntary widowhood as the symbol of love, sacrifice and service. He deplored the treatment and position accorded to widows in Hindu society. He said that every widow has as much right to remarry as every widower. Voluntary widowhood is a priceless boon in Hinduism, enforced widowhood is a curse. No outside imposition can cure Hindu society of the enforced widowhood of girls, who don't even know what marriage is. He never thought that a child widow is a widow in its true perspective. So, he strongly advocated, in the teeth of opposition from the *Sanatana Hindus,* for the remarriages of the so-called widows and quoted from *Sastras* that they are acceptable to reason and dignity of womanhood.

Gandhiji appealed to the women to take a lead in the path of non-violence and peace. He said that God has vouchsafed to women the power of non-violence more than to man. He was of the opinion that India's salvation depends on the sacrifice and enlightenment of her women. He considered women as the other half of man. He never wanted a women to show off their beauty much, but desired that they should raise themselves through dedicated service to the needy. He expected them to derive pleasure in service rather than in procreation.

II

The society of today is like a heap of wheat grains. There are some grains which move to fill up a depression, but their number is small. The other names remain where they are. But the human society we have to build up would be like water. The task of defence and reconstruction of society have got into the clutches of violence and competition. The goddess of defence has taken the form of violence and that of reconstruction the form of competition. The society of today is based on competition. We wish to build up the future society on cooperation. The society stands today on the foundation of ownership. Tomorrow we have to abolish ownership. There are inequalities in the present society. We have to abolish inequalities. Thus we want to build up a new society. We have to transform the present society into a *sarvodaya* one. We have to abolish castes, sects, classes, etc., existing in the society of today. The life of society can be built upon compassionate social structure which is conducive to good.

Vinoba does not want arithmetical equality, but he wants equity, or such equality as, for instance, the five fingers of the hand have. These five fingers are not equal in dimensions, but they all work in full cooperation and together perform innumerable tasks. We want equality tempered with right discrimination. The attempts made in other countries to bring about equality by force lacked the insight of proper discrimination. That is why the idea of equality in those countries is proving abortive. A mother does not distribute food among her childern on the basis of mathematical equality. To the youngest one she gives only milk, to the next some milk and some bread, and to the grown-ups only bread. In the same way, in society also we will exercise discrimination and take into account the intensity of hunger and the power of digestion of each in the distribution of food. Where equality is brought about by force, all are compelled to conform to the same pattern. We are totally against this kind of regimentation. We aim at spiritual equality based on proper discrimination. All differences which make for inequality and disharmony have to be abolished. The differences of rich and poor, of high and low, have been created by man himself.

Varna and *ashrama* are not identical. *Varna* is concerned with social order, which may undergo change. The *varna* system signifies that everybody should discharge his duties in accordance with the social order prevailing at that time. The *ashrama* system is not so much concerned with society as with individuals. There may be some outward changes, but its basic form will remain the same. The organisation of society in terms of hereditary occupational groups is a very great experiment made by Hinduism. But because of the ideas of superiority and inferiority coming into it, its original pure form became contaminated and later through attraction for the principle of economic competition, it became altogether destroyed. That the individual should do the work allotted to him by society, that society should allot him work in view of his fitness, that his inherited dispositions should be taken advantage of in training him into fitness, that having acquired fitness the individual should regard it his duty to take up the work for which he has been trained, that no other should compete with him in his work, that all should receive adequate equal protection and commensurate wages, that all, who do their allotted work with devotion and with a sense of responsibility, should be esteemed equally, and that every individual should work and God be pleased with his worship in the form of doing his own appointed task—such in short is the institution of the hereditary occupational groups.

Varna does not mean caste. There are innumerable castes today in the country and this goes against the original concept of *varnas*. There was a very good idea underlying the four *varnas* formed in India. The idea was that in every *varna* there should be all the four *varnas*. In other words, every person should be a *Brahmin*, a *Kshatriya*, a *Vaishya* and a *Shudra*, and thus be a complete individual. But he should take up the work of one of them only as his social activity. Vinoba wants to say that where there is a peace of mind and heart, it is a mark of a Brahmin. The true mark of a Kshatriya is fearlessness. The third is the *varna* of the Vaishyas. If we have to describe their trait in one word, it will be Kindness. The fourth *varna* is that of the Shudras. If their trait is to be given in a single word, it will be faith.

The idea underlying the *ashram* system is that the purpose of man's life is not the enjoyment of the senses but the service of the world. One has to perceive God by practising self-control. The trait of a *sanyasi* is tranquillity or calmness. Where there is no peace of mind and heart, there is no *sanyas*. One does not become a *sanyasi* by getting his head shaved or by allowing his beard to grow. The test of a *sanyasi* lies in his peace of mind. The next is the stage of *vanaprastha*. Its trait is control over the sense. We have to control them by penance, austerity. We have to attain complete conquest over ourselves. Then comes *Grihasthashram*, the stage of the householder. Its trait is kindness. Lastly there is the stage of *Brahmacharya*. Its trait is faith.

If the householder stage is well-ordered, it results in the proper observance of all the stages of life. A householder needs stability of mind and vital force. It is not that he was a licence for sex indulgence. On the contrary, this *ashram* signifies an endeavour for the purification of mind and heart in an ordered manner and for acquiring training in social service. Love, compassion and tenderness are developed at the stage of a householder. It is needed for these qualities.

At a certain period of life, both husband and wife must give up the responsibility of the house, entrust the same to grown-up children, live like brother and sister, and take to life of public service. If they do not do so, the evolution of the soul is blocked up. The *shastras* enjoin all, who attain the grandfatherly status, tc abandon their homes and to devote themselves to educating the society. There is plenty of education in our country today, but good and experienced teachers are not available.

Sanyasa means the complete elimination of self-regard or self-hood and a sense of unity and harmony with the whole world. A *sanyasi* has no interest of his own; in fact, the words 'I' and 'mine' are not to be found in his dictionary. A *sanyasi* does not give up love. He develops love but gives up jealousy and vices. He relinquishes the house to seek how to make his love universal.

We solemnise marriage with auspicious rites so that it does not become a plaything of lust. The sex desire is present in all living creatures. When it gets perverted, it results in adultery, bloodshed, lack of restraint, indulgence, etc. All these are perversions. There should not only be no perversions, the sex desire should also be sublimated. Parents can advise about marriage, they can help, but it is the decision of the girl herself which must be respected. If the advice of the parents appeals to her, it is all right. If it does not, parents feel distressed over it.

In the Hindu society women are far behind. Besides legal and social hurdles, they also face hindrances created by spiritual notions. There was a time when it was said that they were not entitled to study the *Vedas.* Even the males of today are not interested in this right for themselves. It commands no value. But when it was considered as valuable, women did not have a right to it. Even highly religious persons and the learned ones were of the view that women had no right to observe life-long *brahmacharya.* All this has created a very big spiritual obstacle for them. The result is that the ideal before every girl is, and it is also inculcated in her, that she has to leave her father's house for another. Their whole education is based on it. Their attitude too is moulded accordingly. India does not conceive of independent enterprising women.

The ornaments have made prisoners of women, and society regards them as blessed symbols of wifehood. The importance of wife is no less than that of the husband, but society did not feel the need of prescribing some blessed symbols for him as well. Just as machines have destroyed village industries, foreign countries have destroyed the trade of our cities and our cities have destroyed our village industries, in the same way men have made an organised effort to destroy women's industries. Today we have made the relationship between man and woman artificial. We think that women are protected and men are their protectors. This is a mistake. In our society, women should not be merely protected, she should be capable of self-protection as well.

To quote Vinoba, "I am not inclined to recognise any difference between man and woman. I consider that women's social, family and political rights and responsibilities are exactly the same as men's. Both have equal economic rights, and both have equal moral capacities. They should be educated together and should study the same subjects. Their differences are external, not basic."[9] There is a popular notion that women are more passionate than men, but this is a mistaken idea. Women have to suffer the pains of childbirth and have to face great difficulties for their children's sake. Hence it does not seem that they would have greater liking for that passion because of which they have to undergo so much suffering.

There are some common and some special factors in the education of men and women. The spirit of both men and women is equally pure. In this respect there is no difference between them. This is the first common factor. The second common factor is about 'desires'. Both have common desires like those of hunger and greed. They both bear the same relationship to nature. It is not that nature appears to them differently. This is the third common factor. Thus it is clear that in the education of men and women greater part is common. The laws of the development of qualities apply to them equally. Taking these things into consideration Vinoba says that they should get the same education and both should be educated together.

If there is injustice, cruelty and hatred between husband and wife, children suffer. Under such conditions, there is no harm in recognising the right of divorce. The whole of morality is based on free will, not on compulsion. It does not ordain, it permits. Therefore, a provision for divorce in special circumstances would be considered as justifiable.

REFERENCES

1. *Young India,* 12-3-25.
2. *Ibid.*, 23-4-25.
3. *Ibid.*, 29-9-27.
4. *Ibid.*, 20-10-27.
5. M.K. Gandhi, *Ashram Observances in Action*, pp. 81-90.
6. *Harijan*, 4-3-33.
7. *Ibid.*, 18-10-36.
8. *Ibid.*, 4-4-36.
9. Vinoba, *Women's Power, Sarva Seva Sangh Prakashan,* Varanashi, 1982, pp. 17-18.

5

ECONOMIC THOUGHT OF GANDHI AND VINOBA

Gandhiji had imbibed a rare insight into various problems facing our country to which others could not. His ideas revealed a pragmatic and rational approach, specifically, for the economic problems faced by our country. He did not receive any formal training in economics, nor did he study much economics on his own. However, in technical sense of the term, he was not well acquainted with economics. But his economic ideas were shaped by his own practical experiences and intensive reading of Ruskin, Tolstoy, *Gita* etc. He viewed economics and economic problems in a different way. He insisted that the objective of human conduct should be moral and spiritual development. He had no faith in an economics which is devoid of morality. To him, that economics is untrue which disregards the moral values. True economics stands for social justice and promotes the good of all. True economics never militates against the highest ethical standard and an economics that inculcates mammon worship and enables the strong to amass wealth at the expense of the weak is a false and dismal science. True economics never conflicts with the moral standards, as all true ethics must be also good economics. He considered true economics as indispensable for a decent life. He said, "I do not draw a sharp or any distinction between economics and ethics. Economics that hurt the moral well-being of an individual or a nation is immoral, and therefore, sinful".[1]

The basic principle in determining the course of human history is soul and not the matter. Gandhiji has given a spiritual interpretation of human history. He observed that the essential difference between man and the brute is that the former can respond to the call of the spirit in him, can rise superior to the possessions that he owns in common with the brute.

The spiritual and moral progress made by man during all these centuries, must also be borne in mind in determining, the future course of human history. He remarked that class war is foreign to the essential genius of India. He said that Indian should not be observed with catch-words and seductive slogans imported from the West. They should have faith in their distinct Eastern Tradition. He asked his countrymen to study their Eastern institution in a spirit of scientific enquiry and endeavour to find a solution which promises an escape from the vicious circle of violence and exploitation. He was of the opinion that it is surely wrong to presume that the Western socialism and communism are the last word on the question of mass poverty.

Gandhiji stood for a simple and, more or less, self-sufficient living in rural surroundings. He had an ideal of simple living and high thinking. He stood for voluntary reduction of wants. To him, craze for multiplicity of goods is destructive of contentment, peace and tranquillity. He advocated the establishment of ideal villages in India where the people could pursue the ideal of simple living and high thinking.

Gandhiji wanted to reduce the number of wants to the minimum so that they are satisfied and satisfaction is got in every case and consequently welfare is maximised. If the wants grow in number and some of them cannot be satisfied, pain will be the consequence, reducing the size of welfare. When the purchasing power is limited, it is good to have only few wants and to get them satisfied fully so that pleasure and welfare become positive and maximum. He did not advocate unnecessary reduction in wants. What he wanted was that wants should not become an end in themselves. They are good as long as they can be anyway help in increasing human welfare, but they are to be discarded if they in anyway add unnecessarily to the drudgery of human life. He said that a certain degree of physical harmony and comfort is necessary, but above a certain level it becomes a hindrance instead of help. Therefore, the ideal of creating an unlimited number of wants and satisfying them seems to be a delusion and snare. The satisfaction of one's physical needs, even the intellectual needs of one's narrow self, must meet at a certain point a dead stop, before it degenerates into physical and intellectual voluptuousness. He does not believe that multiplication of wants and machinery contrived to supply them is taking the world a single step nearer its goal.

Gandhiji remarked that western nations are today groaning under the heal of the monster-God of materialism. He said, "I believe that independent India can only discharge her duty towards a groaning world by adopting a simple but ennobled life by developing her thousands of cottages and living at peace with the world. High thinking is inconsistent with complicated material life based on high speed imposed on us by mammon worship".[2] Man falls from the pursuit of the ideal of plain living and high thinking the moment he wants to multiply his daily wants. The human body is meant solely for service, never for indulgence. The secret of happy life lies in renunciation.

To Gandhiji, God created man to work for his food and said that those who ate without work were thieves. He said, "If everybody lives by the sweat of his brow, the earth would become a paradise. . . . If everyone laboured physically for his bread . . . . poets, doctors, lawyers and others would consider it their duty to use those talents gratis for the service of humanity. Their output will be all better and richer for their selfless devotion to duty".[3] He remarked that the great nature has intended us to earn our bread in the sweat of our brow. Everyone, therefore, who idles away a single minute becomes to that extent a burden upon his neighbours, and to do so, is to commit a breach of the very first lesson of *ahimsa*. Bread labour shall be the foremost duty of every member of society. He wanted that everyone should do some sort of manual labour to earn his bread. He believed that bread labour would bring about a steady and silent revolution in society. To him, the needs of the body must be supplied by the body. Intellectual labour could not be a substitute for bodily labour.

According to Gandhiji, "If all laboured for their bread and no more, then there would be no cry of over-population, no disease and no such misery as we see around. Such labour will be the highest form of sacrifice. . . . There will then be no rich and no poor, none high and none low, no touchable and no untouchable. . . . If we did so, our wants would be minimised, our food would be simple. We should then eat to live, not live to eat. . . . Intellectual labour is for the soul and is its own satisfaction".[4] He wanted to stop the mad craze for white collar jobs and check the feeling of hatred towards physical labour. Physical labour done out of ignorance or compulsion cannot be termed as bread labour. He remarked that compulsory obedience to a master is a state of slavery, willing obedience to one's father is the glory of the sonship. Similarly, the compulsory obedience to the law ofbread labour breeds poverty, diesase and discontent. It is a state of slavery. Willing obedience to it must bring contentment and health.

Gandhiji observed, "Intellectual work is important and has an undoubted place in the scheme of life. But what I insist on is the necessity of physical labour. No man, I claim ought to be free from that obligation. It will serve to improve even the quality of his intellectual output".[5] He said, "Thirty-four years of continuous experience and experimenting in truth and non-violence have convinced me that non-violence cannot be sustained unless it is linked to conscious body labour".[6] Being a practical man, he knew that it is an ideal which is difficult to be achieved in the present world. But he felt that it was a good ideal and one must strive to achieve it.

Gandhiji laid great stress on moral and spiritual values. He advocated truth and non-violence as the powerful means to achieve the ultimate goal of life. He often measured economic progress of a country in terms of the moral character and social integrity of its citizens. To him, economics and ethics cannot be divorced; life must be viewed completely and as a whole. Orthodox economics has been laying undue stress on the values of money and material wealth to the exclusion of moral and human values. For him, everybody should be able to get sufficient work to enable him to make the two ends meet. And this ideal can be universally realised only if the means of production of the elementary necessaries of life remain in the control of the masses. He held that the industrialisation instead of employment generation would displace the labour and take work and bread away from millions in this country. He pleaded for *khadi* and village industries.

Gandhiji was against rapid industrialisation of India. He had a great distrust for anything mechanical. He regarded the State as a soulless machine. He explained that the individual has a soul, the state being a soulless machine only represents violence in a concentrated and organised form. He believed that industrialisation would prove to be a curse for mankind, as it depends entirely on the capacity to exploit others. He said, "My fundamental objection to machinery rests on the fact that it is machinery that has enabled these nations, to exploit others".[7] He condemned the mechanisation of the west. He said that machinery is like a snakehole which may contain from one to a hundred snakes. He remarked that he cannot recall a single good point in connection with machinery. He was of the opinion that industrialisation was not necessary for India as her ideal of 'high thinking' was in consistent with European ideal of complicated material life based on mammon worship. He remarked that he was not against machinery as such; he was only opposed to the craze for having devices which plunged millions of people into the abyss of enforced idleness. Regarding the use of machines, in his own words Gandhiji said, "I entertain no fads in this regard. All that I desire it that every able bodied citizen of India should be provided with gainful employment. If electricity or even atomic energy could be used without displacing human labour and creating unemployment, I will not raise my little finger against it. I am, however, still to be convinced that this would be possible in a country like India where capital is scarce and labour abundant."

Gandhiji regarded industrialisation as a curse to mankind. He condemned industrialisation because it accentuates materialism and spreads moral corruption. He said, "Indeed the West has had a surfeit of industrialisation and exploitation. The fact is that this civilisation is all evil . . . . I have no quarrel with steamship and telegraphs. They may stay, if they can without the support of materialism and all it connotates".[8] He remarked, "I would prize every invention of science made for the benefit of all".[9] Every machine that helps every individual has a definite place in society. However, he made it clear that he would not tolerate such machines which might result in the displacement of labour and the centralisation of wealth. He said that he would welcome every improvement in the cottage machine, but he knows that it is criminal to displace hand labour by the introduction of power driven spindles unless one is at the same time ready to give millions of farmers some other occupation in their houses. He remarked that today machinery helps a few to ride on the backs of millions. The impetus behind it all is not the philanthropy to save labour, but greed. It is against this construction of things that he is fighting with all his might.

Gandhiji wanted India to evolve a system of non-violent occupations instead of industrialism. He believed that the large-scale production with its competitive economy would not be compatible with the concept of a society of equal and free. Hence he favours rural economy. Village was to be the basic of economic system. It was to be self-contained and self-sufficing. Mahadev Desai said that the ideal economic condition of a country is not to remain an exploiter of raw products for foreign countries but to be self-contained. The self contained unit will constitute an area covered by a radius of about five miles. Each unit shall have a definite pattern of consumption and a well integrated system of production. The consumption pattern will depend upon the geographical situation of the locality, the temperament of the people, the traditional regulation, economic pattern and upon the educational and cultural attainment of the people.

For Gandhiji, economic exploitation was the essence of violence in society and wars in future could be eschewed only by following bold policy of decentralisation through the organisation of largely self-sufficient village communities. Self-sufficiency does not mean narrowness. Man is as much self-dependent as inter-dependent; when dependence becomes necessary in order to keep society in good order, it is no longer dependence, but becomes cooperation where each is equal to the other. To develop human personality, intelligence, character and artistic senses no centralisation is useful but only decentralisation is advantageous. Centralisation leads to domination and idleness but decentralisation to freedom of the individual and skills with less training make work easy and simple. Decentralisation also leads to self-dependence, mutual respect and sound economic internationalism by avoiding international dependence. In decentralisation production and consumption take place simultaneously avoiding great world tragedy of economic slumps.

Gandhiji wanted the village to produce all that is necessary for the consumption of its own people. Cities should serve as emporia for village products instead of the village being used as a dumping ground for the manufactured goods of the cities. He insisted that the village should be organised not on temporary but on a permanent basis. His idea was the establishment of several independent village units or republics which could manage their own affairs with the least governmental help and outside interference. He said, "Independence must begin at the bottom. Thus, every village will be a republic or panchayat having full powers. . . . it will be an oceanic circle whose centre will be the individual".[10]

Gandhiji wanted to make every village self-supporting for its food and clothing through *khadi*. He conceived *khadi* as an universal industry. *Khadi* ensures the proper utilisation of human labour. *Khadi* would supply work to millions of villages. It would give them hope where but yesterday there were blank despair. According to Gandhiji, spinning must be a compulsory objective of every able bodied man. He conceived spinning as an emblem of non-violence or a doctrine that had its roots in the purest *ahimsa.* He claimed that the revival of spinning would result in the freedom from capitalism and imperialism.

Khadi spirit is the symbol of unit of economic freedom and equality. Decentralisation of the production and distribution of the necessaries of life. Its message is one of simplicity, service of mankind, being so as not to hurt others, creating an indissoluble bond between the rich and the poor, capital and labour, the prince and the pauper. In addition to *khadi,* he mentioned some village industries like hand-grinding, tanning, hand-pounding, soap-making, oil-pressing etc. Without *khadi,* these industries cannot have the existence of their own. He said, "Our clear duty is to investigate the possibilities of keeping in existence the village wheel, the village crusher and the village pounder, and by advertising their products, discovering their qualities, ascertaining the condition of the workers and the number displaced by the power driven machinery and discovering the methods of improving them, while retaining their village character to enable them to stand the competition of the mills".[11]

Gandhiji was against the theory of abolition of private property on the basis of trusteeship. He believed in liquidating class interests by conversion and not by coercion. He was of the opinion that total economic equality was neither possible, nor able to be established. He regarded the individual as the supreme architect of his own government and preferred minimum state or governmental interference in his private and public life. His ideal of *Ramrajya* was based on this. He wanted to revive and re-establish India's old *samaj* ideal based on morality. He pointed out that India could save herself from ruin and stagnation only by reconstructing and revitalising her village and society.

II

An economics which goes against humanity, is not a human economics but a demoniac economics. Principles of economics which can be suitably applied in India, may not suit America or Russia. Even in India, the suitability of certain principles of economics may vary from time to time. In modern economics, the human factor has been reduced and greater attention has been paid to the increase of mechanical power. Vinoba wants to discard money economy, i.e. a social order based on money and to establish in its place an order based on labour.

According to Vinoba, "All Rajas (monarchs) have gone away for good in democracy, but money continues to be on the throne. It rules our life. It is at the basis of our dealings. But it is thoroughly a rougue or villain by character. It resembles a knave through and through. A knave's word cannot be relied upon. So also money's. Sometimes it fetches eight seers of wheat, other times five and hardly two seers at still other times. Consequently integrity is at a discount. Man has exalted money to be the highest status. Hence the more he gets it, the more secure he feels. And since the value of money, like knave's words, is undependable, his passion for money knows no bounds. The higher the passion, the greater the avidity. Thus in all walks of life money enjoys ascendency. Everybody, from peasant to the trader and on to the Brahmin, is mad after it. The government is equally mad after it. Hence it realises revenue in cash and not in kind. It also encourages money crops like tobacco, jute, etc. We have to break this vicious circle and bring down money from the pedestal it enjoys today. Bringing down money, we have to raise the dignity of

Lakshmi (wealth), which is born of productive bodily labour. Money is made at the press in Nasik, you can print any amount of it. But Lakshmi is produced by hard work, toil and sweat".[12] He prefers paper currency provided there is a reference to labour hours on it and not to the money.

As long as economic equality is not established in the country, there would be no peace. It is the economic inequality among the people that is making India unhappy. Political independence would be complete only when it is followed by economic independence. It is therefore, the duty of the people to establish economic equality. By equality Vinoba does not mean absolute equality. Our aim should be to give people all things that are necessary for the maintenance of the body. The luxurious life of the West, which led to greed and wars after wars among nations and created dissatisfaction and unhappiness, should not be the ideal for India.

The development of the attachment for private property in the people is due to the present social structure and laws. A man wants ownership because he desires to live on the labour of others. Private ownership is now being assailed at on one side by self-knowledge and on the other by science. Instead of abolishing private property, Vinoba wants that the emotional involvement with it should go. He also holds that if someone has earned something by his honest efforts, none should attack it. Its expropriation would be wrong. But the word 'property' denotes, one has to see as to how it was acquired, whether the means were proper or improper. If they were not proper, the term 'property' does not apply to it. But if it has been acquired by moral means, it is something sacrosanct. However, if a father earns something by honest labour, we tell him that you are entitled to your earnings but relinquish that right as far as your progeny is concerned. And if he agrees to it, it would not be deemed immoral but moral.

Vinoba agrees that there is no sacredness in private property. But it is equally necessary to understand that forcible expropriation can never end the attachment and greed of man for wealth. The Muslims were great iconoclasts. They broke idols. But what happened? Idolatry has not vanished from our land. If anything, it has become stronger. If they had explained to the people why idolatry was wrong and convinced them that it was meaningless, the result would have been different.

Vinoba said that if power is decentralised while ownership is being maintained, it shall only be a scheme of decentralised exploitation. It should be a prior condition for the membership of cooperative societies that ownership must be relinquished. "A society without vision is a decadent society. Vision gives vitality and strength and inspires a people to noble adventure. It creates the national ethos. Society progresses when its members have a sense of social purpose. No society can survive or hold its head high unless its members have a sense of purpose. Increasing production or the doubling of national income may be necessary but it cannot be called a national objective. Industrial nations of the West have done it. We see that some insects and animals also show an acquisitive instinct. In a poor country like India it is obvious that we need higher production urgently. No one can belittle its importance. And yet it cannot take the place of a national purpose. In spite of economic plenty there is fear and a sense of insecurity in the countries of the West",[13] said Vinoba.

It is argued that the first thing necessary being full production, the problem of distribution may well wait for the present. But this is a mechanical way of reasoning. Mechanical methods might be good in process of production, but their application in logic leads to fallacious thinking. If there were no production at all, there would be no problem of distribution. But since there is some production, the question of proper distribution automatically arises along with it. If, again, distribution could be postponed until full production was reached, perhaps it would be possible to put off its consideration to a later stage. But we do consume day after day whatever is produced. And while some secure far more than what is just, other's don't get enough. And it is the producers who almost invariably get less. If unequal distribution adversely affected non-producers only, there could be perhaps some justification for it. Even if it had been the case that though the non-producers got a larger share, producers were able to get sufficient enough, the consideration of equitable distribution could be deferred. But the present condition does not admit of patient awaiting. Under these circumstances, the issue whether production or distribution should be regarded as more important, is irrelevant and one cannot be preferred to another without harm. Another error involved in such compartmental consideration about the problems of production and distribution is that it might lead to the adoption of such methods of production as to make equitable distribution impossible later on. Our methods of production must be such as to solve the problem of equitable distribution simultaneously with increased production.[14]

Simplicity highly becomes of man. When we lead a simple life, we do not have to devote much attention to the externals. We can concentrate on inner things, we can think none. By simple life is meant ordering of one's life in accordance with the standard prevailing in the society as a whole. More attention should be paid to raising the level of thinking than that of living. No doubt, in a country like India, where people do not even get the necessities of life, the standard of living will have to be raised. But higher thinking is only possible with simple living. Wherever the standard of living is very low, it must be raised, but it should also be realised that happiness does not increase by merely increasing material conveniences or gadgets. It is wrong to think that we shall be happier if there are more goods in the house. Man only derives peace and satisfaction when he keeps away both from comforts and misery.

Decentralisation presupposes a comprehensive all pervading idea behind the various village industries. In the absence of any such idea, small non-centralised industrial units mean merely scattered industries. There were plenty of them before the machine age. But they were easily swept off with the first impact of the machine age. Decentralisation will stand on firm foundation.

It should be comprehended that science and technology are identical. A misconception prevails in this country that science stands for big machines. But this wrong impression should be removed by us. Science means the knowledge of nature. Hence, just as it is utilised in big machines, it can also be used in small ones. Vinoba said, "If the introduction of science and technology helps small tools, I need it. I am in favour of it. The only conditions are that neither should they be monopolised by any particular individual and nor should they result in the exploitation of others. That much precaution would have to be taken. Therefore, when you say that the industrial civilisation is going to have a comprehensive impact on life, I have a feeling that it too is an advance in the same way as there had been from the Greek culture onwards. Such developments always create some problems and it has also happened in this case. However, its solution lies in finding out the purposes for which it can be advantageously used and not in rejecting it altogher".[15]

Machine lacks intelligence. Vinoba accepts those machines which are necessary and reject those which are not. A machine is made for man and must ever remain subservient to him. It must never be permitted to ride over him. He said, "Machines are of three categories, time-saving, destructive and productive. I am not against time-saving machines, such as trains, aeroplanes, etc. Though they do not add to the production of the country, they save time. Destructive machines, such as guns, bombs, etc. have no place in non-violence. We are, therefore, opposed to them. Productive machines are of two varieties, those that are helpful and those that are harmful. Machines that reduce employment are harmful to human beings. Whether a particular machine is harmful or helpful depends upon time, place and circumstances in which it is used. A machine which might be harmful in one country might be helpful in another. A machine which might be helpful at one time might become harmful at another time. So also with change in circumstances no set formula can be laid down to judge whether a machine is harmful or helpful. We therefore, have neither a blind infatuation for machinery nor an irrational opposition to it. Service of man will be the sole criterion for acceptance or rejection of a machine".[16]

Electricity and gas may be used for housework. Vinoba does not want to eschew any kind of power. Only the spirit should be in control of it. Power should serve man and not become his master. It is not enough that it is cheap, even if it is available for cooking. It must be owned by the villagers.

In a vast country like India, the peasants cannot survive by relying on agriculture alone. Village industries are indispensable for the peasant's survival. All those industries whose raw material is produced in the villages and finished articles are used on consumption should be reserved for villages. It is not at all proper to compel a man to undertake physical labour for eight hours a day to earn his living. If such is the condition of village industries, they should be given up. If a strong healthy man cannot maintain himself properly by working for four hours, it is something which cannot be put up with. In a big country like India there is scope for large scale and village industries. But their spheres should be clearly demarcated. Vinoba wants that some industries should be reserved for villages, specially those for which raw material was there in the villages. Village industries come together with *khadi*. *Khadi* alone will not survive without them.

Vinoba said, "I am not surprised that the spinning wheel does not spread rapidly. It is not a new kind of cigarette or tea to attract people. It is a new and revolutionary idea which goes counter to the prevailing current of thought. He alone can spin who has the courage to go against the modern world currents. I do not, therefore, lose hope at the slow progress of spinning wheel; rather I feel all the more earnest in its cause".[17] Khadi seems to cost more than mill-made cloth, but one must think more realistically in terms of social costs. Among the feelings associated with the spinning wheel those of sympathy for the poor, respect for poverty and finding joy in it, are the important ones. Nothing else has the capability of the *charkha* to bring about unity between the rich and poor. Just as a man has a tendency to get violent if he keeps a sword with him, similarly he acquires *composure* of mind by playing a spinning wheel. *Khadi* cannot survive apart from the concept of *gram swaraj*.

Khadi is as indispensable for *swaraj* as it was for country's independence. If the villagers resolve that they will use nothing but cloth made in their own village, *khadi* will never die out.

Vinoba placed an idea before the *khadi* workers. This is about *lok vastra* (People's cloth). It would be produced and consumed in the village itself. There would be no sale and purchase of it outside the village. If a village decides, a unit of 8 to 10 spindle *charkhas* could be operated by electric power. To clothe a population of one thousand it would need a capital of six thousand rupees and a work-force of forty people. They will have to work full-time for different processes. Since the *charkhas* and looms would be operated by power, the cloth produced may not be *khadi* in the strict traditional definition. The capital investment for this should come from the government. But no more government subsidy, as given in *khadi,* would be necessary to run *Lok Vastra.* Today the Government is giving some help to *khadi,* but it makes no secret of the fact that it looks on *khadi* as a relief measure. It does not believe in the principle that *khadi* stands for a way of life.

In this age of science, decentralisation is easy. Power can be decentralised and distributed to villages. The ideal of village self-sufficiency can, therefore, be accepted as a truly modern concept. The idea of self-sufficiency is often misunderstood. It is certainly not opposed to wider cooperation. It need not be an isolating factor. Vinoba desires that the people should cooperate consciously on as wide a scale as possible. Self-sufficiency enables man to cooperate intelligently with as many groups in the world as he can. From the village republic to the world government there can be a continuous and widening sphere of intelligent cooperation in which all will help one another. Our concept is not a narrow self-sufficiency, but of kindness and compassion. We want to build up a society in which the villages will be self-sufficient. Their daily needs like food, cloth, etc., will be produced in the village itself through small industries. The big industries which have dealings not only all over the country but also with other parts of the world, will not be owned by any individual but by the society.

Cooperation is an eternal principle of life. But it is only when it is given voluntarily and with full knowledge that it is useful and that it is non-violent, and only then it is true cooperation. On the other hand, a cooperation given because of helplessness or ignorance is not of any use to a good state, for though it may look outwardly like cooperation it cannot long because of its unreality. It will develop first into hidden violence and then assuredly into open violence. Vinoba says that the only practical and fruitful way for India is to allow small holdings which individual families of peasants can concentrate their efforts on and produce maximum food-grains through intensive cultivation. He does not insist on collective farming. We should not forget the deplorable economic condition of the country when we discuss economic holding. We have very limited land in our country. The right remedy lies not in increasing the size of holdings, but in resorting to intensive cultivation in small plots of land and increasing yield per acre.

In the ideal state, every individual will receive equal protection. Service from each will be according to his ability and will therefore be unequal. To obtain equal protection is not the same as receiving equal wages. But the inequality which prevails in wages today will under no circumstances exist. Wages will be as little unequal as possible, or to put it positively, will be commensurate. Inequality of wages will not be in proportion to inequality of service, but in proportion to inequality of need. The total amount of service rendered by individuals and the total amount of protection given to them by the state will be equal to each other.[18]

Regarding the ideal village, Vinoba said, "First the dispute in the village should be settled locally in the village. Secondly, you must arrange for providing medical help to all those who may be out of health. Medicines are not to be purchased from outside. Herbs with medicinal properties should be grown in the village and patients should be given their fresh juice and treated with other nature cure methods to restore them to health. Thirdly, we must provide for the education of the village children. All the children in the village should be enabled to receive education and not only those, as at present, who can afford. The fourth constituent of *gramdharma* is agriculture or the service of land. Land will not be owned privately in as much as it belongs to God. All must live and work in cooperation with one another for the good of life. They should lift up the declining village industries and make them prosperous. Every need of the village must be produced or manufactured in the village. Nothing should be brought from outside. Fifthly, there should not be any privately owned shop in the village. All village shops will be held jointly by all the villagers who will have each a share in its capital. These are some of the principles of *gramdharma* or villagism".[19]

REFERENCES

1. R.K. Prabhu and Rao (Eds), *The Mind of Mahatma Gandhi*, Navajeevan Publishing House, Ahmedabad 1966, p. 264.
2. *Harijan*, 1-9-46.
3. *Mahatma*, Vol. VII, 1953, p. 389.
4. *Harijan*, 29-6-35.
5. *Ibid.*, 23.2.47.
6. *Ibid.*, 27.1.40.
7. N.K. Bose, *Selections from Gandhi*, Navajeevan Publishing House, Ahmedabad, 1948, p. 63.
8. *Young India*, 7-10-26.
9. *Harijan*, 22-6-35.
10. *Ibid.*, 28-7-46.
11. *Ibid.*, 19-8-34.
12. *Ibid.*, 8-1-55.
13. *Bhoodan*, 20-2-57.
14. *Harijan*, 12-2-50.
15. *Vinoba Chintan* No. 5, 38.
16. *Harijan*, 5-9-53.
17. *Ibid.*, 17-10-48.
18. Bharatan Kumarappa, *Swaraj Sastra*, Padma Publications Ltd., Bombay, 1945, pp. 52-54.
19. *Harijan*, 5-6-54.

6

POLITICAL THOUGHT OF GANDHI AND VINOBA

The word *swaraj* is a sacred word, a vedic word meaning self-rule and self-restraint and not freedom from all restraints which independence often means. *Swaraj* could be of two types—personal and national. Personal *swaraj* means ruling over oneself. It further means the minimum rules of the Government over the people and the society. The individual will rule over himself in such a way that he will not come in the way of others. He shall be guided by the principles of self-restraint and thereby developing his personality. National *swaraj* means national self-rule and self-restraint in political, economic, social and moral fields.

The concept of *swaraj* has multi-dimensional aspects. Political aspect of *swaraj* means that the superiority of the people over political institutions. Thus in a *swaraj* state, the ultimate power would be decentralised and vested with the people. Hence there is no scope for political domination by any group. *Poorna swaraj* in its political sense will mean the sharing of the fruits of all without discrimination and hindrance. National economic *swaraj* means availability of food, cloth and shelter for all. The village should be self-sufficient in basic necessities. *Poorna swaraj* in economic sense can be achieved only by fulfiling the above and there will be no scope for economic exploitation and domination. The social aspect of national *swaraj* implies the removal of social suppression of the community by another. It means removal of untouchability, social inequality, lack of peaceful co-existence, social hierarchy. Social *swaraj* will be complete only if due place is given for women in the society. With regard to the moral aspect of *swaraj*, full moral height can be achieved only through non-violence. It connotes that the moral development of the man and the state goes hand in hand.

In the Gandhian terminology, the *swaraj* of a people means the sum total of the *swaraj* of the individuals. National *swaraj* is the sum total of all activities which would build an ideal state based on moral force. Gandhiji said that the real *swaraj* will come not by the acquisition of authority by a few but by the acquisition of capacity by all to resist authority when abused. So in a predominantly non-violent society the state will govern the least and use the least amount of force. Self-government means continuous efforts to be independent of government control whether it is foreign government or whether it is national. *Swaraj* government will be a sorry affair if people look up to it for the regulation of every detail of life. Where this condition does not exist, the government is democratic only in name rather than in spirit.

To quote Gandhiji, "*poorna swaraj* is the common sacred possession of all of us—'*Poorna*' complete because it is as much for the prince as for the peasant, as much for the rich land-owner as for the landless tiller of the soil, as much for the Hindus as for the Musalman, as much for the Parsis and Christians as for the Jains, Jews and Sikhs, irrespective of any distinction of caste or creed or status in life. The very connotation of the word and the means of its attainment to which we are pledged — truth and non-violence — precludes all possibility of that *swaraj* being more for some one than for the other, being partial to some one and prejudicial to the other. Truth and non-violence leave no room for fraud and falsehood .... *swaraj* under this method, therefore, big or small but by ensuring even-handed justice and fair treatment to all".[1]

Gandhiji's dream of village *swaraj* is highly comprehensive and progressive, very much in tune with the Indian social set-up. As a practical man, having clear and realistic perception of problems of Indian villages, he had made concrete efforts for its overall upliftment. He considered village *swaraj* as an ideal, to be achieved for the true liberation of Indian masses.

Gandhiji stood for the establishment of a stateless democracy based on truth and non-violence. Decentralised administration was the core of his thinking and his concept of 'state' was the ultimate goal of *sarvodaya* social order. The basis of Gandhian state is the active cooperation of the people. The social structure of Gandhian state is founded on the moral ideal of self-realisation which inspires and moulds the conception of life in all spheres. He found an easy approach to his ideal of decentralised society in villages. Ideally, he opposed 'state' in all its forms and stood for a stateless society thereby qualifying himself as a philosophical anarchist.

Gandhiji rejected the idea of state chiefly on ethical and moral ground. State is deeply rooted in violence and perpetuates exploitation. Hence he was for its abolition. He viewed state as opposed to the nature of man. He defined man in certain moral and spiritual terms. To him, man is not merely a mass of bones and flesh but something more. There is also a spirit, a soul in him which is though, invisible but is all pervading and self-conscious and is a part and parcel of God.

State retards the growth of individual's personality and is destructive to his freedom. So, Gandhiji views every increase in the power of the state with fear. To him, the individual is one supreme consideration. He is an end in himself and the state acts just as a vehicle in and through which the individual realises his best self. He regarded the individual as an architect of his own government. Political power is not an end in itself but one of the means of enabling people to better their condition in every department of life. The state represents force and violence as such and is inconsistent with the nature of man. Violence checks and arrests the development of his moral life. The state hinders his development and stifles his individuality.

Gandhiji did not regard political power as divine punishment imposed on man due to his fall. Nor did he regard political institutions as the revelation of some universal reason, nor as a bourgeois institution or an agency of exploitation of labour by the capitalists. He was repelled by violent nature of the state. He hoped that people are the roots, the state is the fruit. If the roots are civic, the fruits are bound to be civic.

The ideal society of Gandhiji is a stateless society. In it there shall be no railway, no police, no military, no law courts. In short, it will be free from all the complexities of modern state. In it the life shall be simple, easy and free. It would be an ordered anarchy or a state of enlightened anarchy. In such a state everyone is his own ruler. He rules himself in such a manner that he is never a hindrance to his neighbour. In it there is no political power, because there is no state. In practice, however, he realised that such an ideal was difficult to be realised. He believed that a state can be administered on a non-violent basis if the vast majority of the people are non-violent.

Gandhiji favoured representative from of Government. In his book, *Hind Swaraj*, he characterished the British Government as a sterile woman and prostitute-sterile because unproductive and not beneficial and prostitute because not loyal and having no master. He was not opposed to the system of election and representation. He said that if independence is born non-violently all the component parts will be voluntarily interdependent working in perfect harmony under a representative central authority which will derive its sanction from the confidence reposed in it by the component parts. He favoured a small number of representatives whose election as well as removal would depend upon the will of the people. The small size shall be plausible due to decentralisation of the political and economic power, the minimisation of the functions of state and the prevalence of small, self-sufficient and self-sustained village units. He suggested indirect election through the village panchayat.

Gandhiji said that there are seven hundred thousand villages in India. Each would be organised according to the will of its citizens, all of them voting. Then there would be seven hundred thousand votes. Each village, in other words, would have one vote. The villages would elect their district administrations and the district administrations would elect the provincial administrations, and these in turn would elect a President who would be the national chief executive.

Gandhiji advocated a high degree of political decentralisation. He said that our capacity for *swaraj* depends on our capacity for solving without reference to, or intervention of the government. Self-government means continuous effort to be independent of government control whether it is foreign or whether it is national. He believed that there are certain things which cannot be done without political power, but there are numerous other things which do not at all depend upon political power. He pleaded for the minimisation of the functions of the state. Whatever functions be allowed to state, must be performed with the employment of the minimum force. He considered that in the non-violent state, 'a small force' will be necessary.

Gandhiji had a very distinct concept of police. Its rank will be composed of deliverers of non-violence. They will be servants and not masters of the people. The people instinctively render them every help and through mutual cooperation they will easily deal with the even decreasing disturbances. However, the functions of the police will be confined to deal with the robbers and dacoits. He would also allow the policemen to carry arms to arrest the lunatics, etc. who are bent upon murder. Likewise, he would permit the methods to prevent crimes, like tear-gas. But he would allow its use only when the condition become such that the use of methods is inevitable. It will be seen as such that he is not against the police but its present form and its through and through violent character. Our inability to do without the police is definitely a sign of our weakness and failure.

Gandhiji had presented his views on military, which focus on non-violence. It may be observed that until 1931, he was in favour of retaining military; but later on, he did not favour it either to maintain civil liberty or internal order. In the non-violent state the defence shall be decentralised. Villages and even the individuals would be capable of defending their liberties against the whole world. He was in favour of a non-violent army.

Gandhiji had outlined the nature and functions of judiciary under a non-violent state. There shall be laws and law courts under *swaraj*, but they will be the guardian and custodians of the liberty of the people. Regarding the courts, he held that they foster public good. The object of law courts is the permanence of the authority of government and in as much as they support the authority of an unjust government, the courts are not the guardians of nation's liberty but the crushing houses to crush a nation's spirit. He considered mutual settlement as the best system of justice for only the parties concerned known in their hearts of hearts who is right and who is wrong. He opined that justice should be cheap and quick. He favoured the arbitration method. Decision of panchayat should be accepted as final except in case of corruption and mishandling of law. Intermediary course be minimised. Case laws should be abolished and the general procedure should be simplified.

Gandhiji considered crime as a mental disease and like any other malady, is the product of prevailing social system. So, he wanted that all crimes, whether big or small, should be treated as disease. As such he suggested that jails should be turned into reformatory centres and workshops. The function of the authorities should be to investigate the causes of the disease, and to cure them. Their outlook should be that of physicians and nurses in a hospital, so that the prisoners may feel that the officials were their friends and they were there to help him and not to harass them in any way.

The non-violent state will be highly decentralised. Decentralisation means the rule by the small, independent, self-sufficing village communities. A society based on non-violence can only consist of groups settled in villages in which voluntary cooperation, is the condition of dignified and peaceful existence. To Gandhiji, village is the main unit in *swaraj*. The village will be independent and complete republic. It shall be self-sufficing as far as possible. Every village's first concern will be to grow its own food crops and cotton for its cloths. It should have a reserve for its cattle, recreation and playground for adults and children. Then if more land is available, it will grow useful money crops, thus excluding *Ganja*, *Tobacco, Opium* and the like. The village will maintain a village theatre, school and public hall. It will have its own water works ensuring clean water supply. Education will be compulsory up to the final basic course. As far as possible, every activity will be conducted on the cooperative basis. The village will be governed by a village panchayat consisting of persons elected annually by the adult villagers. The village communities will function on cooperative basis. Each village community will be a true democracy.

To quote, Gandhiji, "In this structure composed of innumerable villages life will be ever widening never ascending circles. Life will not be a pyramid with the apex sustained by the bottom. But it will be an oceanic circle whose centre will be the individual always ready for the circle of the village, till at least the whole becomes one life composed of individuals, never aggressive in their arrogance but ever humble sharing the majesty of the oceanic circle of which they are integral units".[2]

The village panchayat would undertake maximum functions. The main functions of the panchayat is to revive the industry and to teach the people to avoid disputes. Gandhiji expected the panchayat to be vigilant and a body to induce the sense among the individuals. He suggested the following civic rules for the effective functioning of the panchayat:[3]

1. No panchayat should be set up without the written sanction of a provincial Congress committee;
2. A panchayat should in the first instance be elected by a public meeting called for this purpose;
3. It should be recommended by the Tehsil committee;
4. Such panchayats should have no criminal jurisdiction;
5. It may try civil suits if the parties to them refer any matter to the panchayats;
6. No one should be compelled to refer any matter to panchayats;
7. No panchayat should have any authority to impose fines, the only sanction behind its civil decrees being its moral authority, strict impartiality and the willing obedience of the parties concerned;
8. There should be no social or other boycott for the time being;
9. Every panchayat will be expected to attend to (a) the education of boys and girls in the village, (b) its sanitation, (c) its medical needs, (d) the upkeep and cleanliness of village wells and ponds, and (e) the uplift of and the daily wants of the so-called untouchables;
10. A panchayat that fails without just cause to attend to the requirements mentioned in clause (9) within six months of the election, or fails otherwise to retain the goodwill of villages, or stands self-condemned for any other cause, appearing sufficient to provincial Congress committee, may be disbanded and another

> be elected in its place. The disability to impose fines or social boycott is a necessity of the case in the initial stages, social boycott in villages has been found to be a dangerous weapon in the hands of ignorant or unscrupulous men. Imposition of fines too may lead to mischief and defeat the very end in view. Where a panchayat is really popular and increases its popularity by the constructive work of the kind suggested in clause (9) it will find its judgement and authority respected by reason of its moral prestige and that surely is the greatest sanction anyone can possess and of which one cannot be deprived.

Gandhiji visualised a genuine democracy based on non-violent, and individual freedom in the fashion of true democratic model. Self-government, Self-management, Mutual cooperation all could be practised and developed for better if man lived in small communities. To him, the realisation of Panchayatraj would mean the rule of justice, the rule of all. The multiplicity of functions which the modern state performs will also become unnecessary in the non-violent state due to the simplicity of life, decentralisation and the absence of violent class-conflict and militarism.

Democracy must in essence mean the art and science of mobilising the entire physical, economic and spiritual of all the various sections of the people in the service of the common good of all. Democracy stands for that form of government in which all the classes of people have a voice in the act of government. It means the rule of the people particularly the common or poor people. It is a form of government in which people rule themselves. There is only one class. So it means self-rule. Democracy necessarily means a conflict of will and ideas, involving some times a war to the knife between different ideas.

The first element in the Gandhian theory of democracy is the rights of the minority. The next element is the emphasis on decentralisation and the third element is the pursuit of moral criteria. The true test of democracy is that it attempts to replace force by social will. Gandhiji lays much stress on the essence and spirit of democracy. The spirit of democracy is not a mechanical thing to be adjusted by abolition of forms. It requires change of the heart. The spirit of democracy cannot be established in the midst of terrorism, whether governmental or popular. The first basic principle is the sovereignty of the people based on pure moral authority. He said that democracy is an impossible thing until power is shared by all. Even a *pariah,* a labourer will have his share in self-government. The dignity and worth of human person is the essence of democratic policy is the second principle emphasised by Gandhiji. To him, a born democrat is a born disciplinarian. Democracy comes naturally to him who is habituated normally to yield willing obedience to all laws, human or divine. A democrat must be utterly selfless. He must think and dream not in terms of self or of party, but only of democracy. The true democrat is he who with purely non-violent means defends his liberty and, therefore, his country's and ultimately that of the whole of mankind.

Gandhiji laid down a moral basis for democracy. He said that the lust for power is one of the dangers to democracy. Yet another principle is the non-violence. The science of non-violence alone can lead one to pure democracy and that without the recognition of non-violence on a national scale there can be no such thing as a constitutional or democratic government. His ideas of democracy is that under it, the weakest should have the some opportunity as the strongest. The true democrat defends his personal freedom, the national freedom and the freedom of mankind through the means of non-violence, and democracy and violence cannot go together. The fourth principle is that secularism and democracy are closely related to each other. He held that religion and state should be separated.

The success of democracy depends upon the selection of representatives. To quote Gandhiji, "Fifteen hundred delegates jealous of the interests of the people, broad minded and truthful, would any day be a better safeguard for democracy than six thousand irresponsible men chosen anyhow. To safeguard democracy the people must have keen sense of independence, self-respect and their oneness, and should insist upon choosing as their representatives only such persons as are good and true".[4] He wanted that the voters should be self-respecting and have a sense of oneness. And the representatives should be broad-minded, truthful and interested in the welfare of the people.

Gandhiji believed in qualified adult franchise. He said that lunatics, loafers, very old people and very young people should not have the right to vote. He did not use precisely this language as far as education is concerned but he said that after excluding lunatics, loafers, very old and very young people, others should be allowed to vote, but before that they should be elected. With regard to adult franchise, Gandhiji said, we exclude the young who have not attained maturity. We exclude them because we know that the young are mentally immature and they cannot be expected to understand the problems that face them, they do not know where their interests lie, they do not know whom they should have as their representative and they do not know where their interest lie, they do not know whom they should have as their representative and they do not know who will identify personal interests with those of the society. He held the view that if we allow the launatics, loafers and the uneducted people to exercise their franchise, violence will be there.

Gandhiji said, "For one like me, wedded to non-violence, constitutional or democratic government is a distant dream so long as non-violence is not recognised as a living force, on inviable creed, not a mere policy. While I prate about universal non-violence my experiment is confined to India. If it succeeds, the world will accept it without effort".[5]

Gandhiji remarked that military force is dangerous antithesis to the free growth of the soul and, hence it will be a poor democracy that depends for its existence on military assistance. To him, there is a radical incompatibility between evolution of democracy and the dependence upon the police and the army. Hence a true democracy must cease to rely on the army. He said, "Do not depend on military and the police help. You have to uphold democracy, and democracy and dependence on the military and the people are incompatible". He said that in the case of emergency, the government may take by force the wealth of the individuals but that in such cases the minimum of force has to be applied. There is no exercise of force in his democracy.

Gandhiji criticised the Western democracy. He was opposed to the procedures and practices of British Parliamentary democracy. He considered the British Parliament as sterile and barren. He further commented the Parliament as a talking shop. He condemned Western democratic politics because they were infected with threefold contradiction. Firstly, they believed in the limitless expansion of capitalism. He censured the vindicative imperialism and ruthless repression carried on in Asia and Africa by the so-called democracies. He said that Western democracy as it functions to-day is undiluted Nazism or Fascism. At best it is merely a cloack to hide the Nazi and the Fascist tendencies of imperialism. He is a severe critic of imperialism. Secondly, he criticised the policies of racialism. Finally he held that the Western democracies were dominated by the ruling classes. He said that America is owned by a few capitalist owners. The same is true of South Africa. The people of Europe have no doubt political power, but no *swaraj*. Because of these three contradictions, he said that the European democracies are to his mind a negation of democracy.

Gandhiji was critic of democratic majority. He wanted a democratic government where individual liberty and freedom of opinion and action would be scrupulously protected and even the minority would be not coerced but only persuaded, respected and converted. He said, "I can conceive the possibility of non-violent social ostracism under certain extreme conditions when a defiant minority refuses to bend to the minority, not out of any regard for principle but from sheer defiance or worse. But that time this was certainly not arrived".[6] He held that the minority should also be given opportunities in decision-making. Real democracy, to him, is the way of approaching a question not by examining the numerical strength of those behind the opinion, but by examining the soundness of the opinion on merits. Or else we will never reach a solution even if we reach one, it will be a blind solution simply because it is the wish of the largest body. If the largest body does wrong, it is up to me to say you are wrong and not to submit. The rule of majority does not mean that it should suppress the opinion of even an individual, if it is sound.

The case of majority rule had little meaning for Gandhiji as his objective was to promote the good of both the majority and the minority. He said that no school of thought can claim a monopoly of right judgement. We are all liable to err and are often obliged to revise our judgement. And the least, therefore, that we owe to ourselves as to others is to try to understand the opponent's view-point, and if we cannot accept it, respect it as fully as we expect him to respect ours. It is one of the indispensable tests of healthy public life. The right of dissent is the salt of democracy. He remarked that in matters of conscience, the law of majority has no place. He explained that democracy was not a state in which the people acted like sheep. Under democracy, liberty of opinion and action was jealously guarded. He, therefore, believed that the minority had a perfect right to act differently from the majority. The exercise of the right to discent can take the form of direct non-violent action, the self-suffering process must be to convert the majority to the minority view.

The process of election of the representatives and also the mode of their operation promotes and foments only dissent and division, to the line of the majority. Gandhiji believed in the immutable maxim that Government of the people is possible only so long as they consent either consciously or unconsciously to be governed. He felt that power belongs to the people. He said that a superficial study of British history had made us think that all power percolates to the people from parliament. The truth is that power resides in the people and it is entrusted for the time being to those whom they may choose as their representatives. Parliaments have no powers or even existence independently of the people. Public opinion is the basis of democratic government and, so, he held that legislation in advance of public opinion has often been demonstrated to be futile. He would not consider all legislation passed by the representative assemblies as the coercive apparatus of the ascendant classes. He said that legislation imposed by people upon themselves is non-violence to the extent it is possible in society.

Gandhiji emphasised the importance of education in democracy. He said that in democracy even pure men may unconsciously given wrong decisions. The remedy is more and purer education, greater awakening of the public and in such quickened atmosphere the rise of a number of public workers whose sole duty will be to speak, write and act so as to serve as bright examples for the public. He wanted that the members of the governing group should lead a simple life. He believed that the moralisation of democracy meant the cultivation of the sentiments of sympathy, fellow-feeling and freedom bigotry. In other words, the moralisation of the democratic process meant that cultivation of spiritual humanism. Tolerance is one of the essential basis of democratic political philosophy. He said that the evolution of democracy is not possible if we are not prepared to hear the other side. We shut the doors of reason when we refuse to listen to our opponents, or having listened, make fun of them. If intolerance becomes a habit, we run to risk of missing the truth. Whilst, with the limits that nature has put upon our understanding, we must always keep an open mind and be ever ready to find that what we believed to be truth was, after all untruth. This openness mind strengthens the truth in us.

Gandhiji wanted India to evolve 'True Democracy' and laid down six conditions for its realisation in India—*satyagraha* expressed through the *charkha*, growth of village industries, primary education through handicrafts, removal of untouchability, communal harmony, and non-violent organisation of labour.

Democracies are no longer the governments of the people even for it is *dandasakti* or the power of coercive violence, and not real *jansakti* or the power of people, that actually sustains them. The modern democracies receive their ultimate sanction only from their standing armies. *Rajniti* is the politics of power, while *Lokniti* is the politics of the people. *Rajniti* means strengthening the power of the state as the chief instrument of social welfare. As against this, *Lokniti* encourages self-support and initiative on the part of the people and wants them to promote their own welfare through voluntary institutions. While *Rajniti* is the embodiment of administration from without, *Lokniti* emphasises the development of self-control and self-discipline from within. In *Raajniti*, people compete for the acquisition of power, whereas in *Lokniti* there is an anxiety to develop the civic character of society through services and cooperation.

The former results in an emphasis on right, the latter lays stress on the proper performance of duties. Evidently the aim of politics of a democratic set-up should itself be to evolve into *Lokniti*.

As pointed out by Vinoba, *Lokniti*, as a matter of fact is simultaneously a way of life, a form of social order and a method of action. As a way of life, it stands for the self-regulation of individual conduct and for a habit to act on one's own initiative. As a form of social order, it envisages a society in which police and military will have little to do and the law will interfere least with life. A man will have the utmost freedom of action but will not abuse it for the social order will be such as to discourage and encourage the social tendencies in him. As a method, it stands for social change in a manner that would maintain man's freedom of action. In other words, it would be brought through conversion and not coercion, through persuasion and not suppression.

Gandhiji never believed in theorising disarmament. His concern was more for the need to develop positive attitude towards disarmament and to work for inducing a preparedness for accepting a non-violent way of life as a universal principle. He said that if the mad race for armament continues it is bound to result in slaughter such as has never occurred in history.

Gandhiji considered war as an expression of violence in an aggressive fashion thwarting economic justice, soverign equality and peaceful cooperation among the nations. His suggestion for establishing world peace are third party settlement, complete disarmament, *shanti sena* and world government. He said that actual process of war is unrighteous because it contradicts *ahimsa* and the higher law of *dharma*. In his opinion voluntary efforts should act as the effective means for disarmament. Such efforts should be based on living faith in truth and non-violence and high degree of sincerity. He was sure that all nations cannot disarm all of a sudden. Hence he stated that some nations will have to dare to disarm herself, and take large risks. The level of non-violence in that nation, if that event happily come to pass, will naturally have risen so high as to command universal respect. Her judgement will be unerring, her decision will be firm, her capacity for heroic self-sacrifice will be great and she wants as much for other nations as for herself. Peace will not come out of the clash of arms but out of justice lived and done by unarmed nations in the face of odds.

Gandhiji suggested world government as a means to establish peace and disarmament. Such a world order has to be essentially based on faith in non-violence. It needs more of self-discipline, education and training to restructure the existing order and to establish a moral and non-violent sanction. But he cautioned that internationalism is possible only when nationalism becomes a fact. Establishment of a Peace Brigade can be highly supportive to the maintenance of such a world order. It can avoid the undue expenditures incurred on the militarisation and at the same time promote the message of peace in a more effective and non-violent way.

Another means to reach the goal of disarmament is 'Decentralisation'. Power corrupts and absolute power corrupts absolutely. When the political, economic and social fields are distributed in the decentralised manner foreign invasion is unlikely. The administrative set-up gains more solidarity and alertness in a decentralised organisational set-up.

Addition of weapon is not a guarantee of security, rather, it can lead to greater threat and insecurity. Had the physical power been effective in regulating life and bringing peace, nuclear weapons could have been effective to enrich the world with peace and harmony. The experience gained from the history proves it to be otherwise. Hence, Gandhiji stressed on the importance of building of moral basis for human life. Moral strength and mutual respect leads to solidarity and aims at means thereby reducing the tensions and crisis.

Gandhiji stressed very much on the need and importance of internal harmony for national and world peace. He considered it as a pre-requisite for a harmonious non-violent life. The internal security and solidarity will ensure better prospects for peaceful living as it does not have to depend on armed forces. To quote Pyarelal, "Such a nation would not excite the envy and greed that ostentatious concentration of wealth excites or become the victim of aggression, because it would command the goodwill and sympathy of all".

Dependence leads to insecurity in many respects. A country can be free from the threat of invasion only when it can support itself for the basic needs. Reliance on foreign goods open the channel for exploitation. Hence Gandhiji gave much importance to the concept of *swadeshi* and self-sufficiency. He realised that a self-contained society need not become a slave or need not ply for external help. Hence more prospects for internal harmony. This made him to convey the message that self-sufficiency is a key to non-violence and disarmament.

For achieving the ideal goal of disarmament, efforts have to be made at all levels. The most basic change should commence from the individual heart, extended to international outlook for world peace. Gandhiji's views on disarmament cannot be kept aside nor can they be considered utopian. His approach to resist violence and promote non-violence can only usher the real welfare and development of the world today.

There are various measures adopted to re-establish peace on the earth. But it is conveniently forgotten that true peace can inhere in minds that are free from the tussels of life and seriously contrasting social set-up. The human nature has moved in the direction of simple to complex and it has now to march backward to simplicity to attain the true peace in human life. Gandhiji offered the concept of peace brigade *(shanti sena)* in this connection. Many could not understand or appreciate the concept and its developmental value.

By establishment of *shanti sena,* Gandhiji desired to organise a non-violent force to intervene in the conflicting situation, to root out the causes of violence and peacelessness and to establish a society dominated by peace, characterised by truth and non-violence. He considered it as a means to build up a *sarvodaya* society. The idea of *shanti sena* has not only a conflict resolving purpose but also it works as a constructive force for the all-round development of the society. He said that *shanti sena* acts unlike armed men, as well in times of peace disturbances. They would be constantly engaged in constructive activities and make riot impossible. There will be the duty of seeking occasions for bringing warring communities together carrying on peace propaganda engaging in activities that would bring and keep them in touch with every single person, male and female, adult and child, in the perish or division. Thus, it has a developmental and preventive value embodied within it.

On 18th March, 1938, Gandhiji enunciated the concept of *shanti sena* through *Harijan.* As a follower of Gandhi ideology, Vinoba realised the importance of it. During his southern tour, he established the first unit on 27th August, 1957. Gradually the concept and message of *shanti sena* spread over to various parts of the country. Subsequently, many peace centres were established.

The outline of the structure of *shanti sena* is also specified. The membership should not be very large, that is, the size of the non-violent corps will be small yet efficient. The members should contact with the local people and establish good rapport with them. As the members hail from the same locality, their relation with the society is cordial and intimate. Membership should not be based on physical fitness, but should be based on character. They may wear badges for identity, preferably of yellow colour and should be in white uniform. They should not carry weapon but should have the knowhow of first aid and fire-fighting. A peace soldier should cultivate the art of silence. They should be trained for practising *brahmacharya.*

Functionally, *shanti sena* has two aspects — 'seva' and 'shanti'. Vinoba said that *shanti sena* will help the poor. It will try to get rid of individual land ownership. It will give personal service to sick. It will try to increase productivity in the village. It will arrange for education. There will be no dissension in the village if the *shanti sena* serves it in these ways. It will be the *shanti sena* task to destroy the root cause of unrest-the gulf between the haves and have-nots, cruelty, the pride of ownership, the insistence on mine and thine, on high and low, on caste distinctions, on religious differences and disputes.

It is neither the duty nor is it possible for a Peace Soldier to find a solution for all problems. He has to resist in times of riots and violence. Functionally they can substitute the police. If there are previous warnings of storm, they could prepare themselves to deal with the situation. Sometimes, the full-time workers are also suggested. At other times, the workers should have sufficient leisure to serve the purpose. The maintenance of the *shanti sena* should be out of the funds collected by means of *sampatidan*. The number does not matter, but it is more of the spiritual and moral preparedness and sacrificial attitude that is more important. Devotional songs and *bhajan* with the assistance of musical instruments can help such peace workers. Sufficient training schools should be established for preparing the peace workers. Refresher programmes are also useful.

It is necessary for a peace soldier to cultivate the social service outlook and be fully prepared to help the people in danger and distress. They should discipline the mind through spiritual and moral ways and should uphold the qualities a of true worker with firm faith in truth and *ahimsa.* Then only they can succeed in their task of serving the society for maintaining the peace. Lord Mountbatten's tributes to Gandhiji as 'one man boundary force' is not an exaggeration when we consider the living faith of Gandhiji in the power of truth and non-violence.

II

Self-Government means ruling over oneself. It follows that we shall have *Swaraj* when all people have acquired the strength of self-control and have realised their duties. Until then we have only government. It is one mark of *Swaraj* not to allow any outside power in the world to exercise control over oneself. And the second mark of *swaraj* is not to exercise power over any other. These two things together make *swaraj* - no submission and no exploitation. Under *swaraj* the smallest child will have the strength to stand against the whole society to declare its resolve not to suffer injustice. The society in which even a person who lacks physical strength stands firmly to express his independent opinion against the whole of it for the protection of morality, is free. Every adult person, whether great or small, has now one vote for himself. But conferring the right of vote in itself does not mean *swaraj*. *Swaraj* will come into being when all are valued equally, all are honoured equally and all are socially held equal. But *swaraj* of this kind does not exist in any country of the world.

The self-government has two aspects. One is of the decentralised power, i.e. the whole power be distributed among the villages and the affairs of a village should be conducted by the villagers themselves. The second is of giving such education, inculcating such psychology and teaching such philosophy as are against that in the power of violence. We must devote ourselves to building up an independent people's power *(Lok-shakti),* and that in itself will be our true service both to the government and to the nation. By an independent people's power Vinoba means a power inhering in the people, which is totally opposed to the power of violence, but is other than the power of the law, and which it must be our task to call into being. We have handed over the power of the law to our government, and although it contains an element of coercion, we regard it as being in a different class from out and out violence because society as a whole has conferred these legal powers on the government. It is our task to create a situation in the country in which there will be no need to use even these sanctions of the law. If we can do that we shall have fulfilled our own true *dharma.*

The State exists merely to apply to the whole society the economic principle which is found everywhere to a greater or less extent in the family. This is the task beyond the power of the family. If the state does not do this service, there is no need for its existence. If instead of performing this service it produces economic inequality it will be right to destroy it and to establish anarchy. Administrators have spread fear of anarchy everywhere in order to make people submit meekly to their rule, however bad it may be.

Three different theories of government are before us. The first is that the state will ultimately wither away and be transformed into a stateless system; but in order to bring it about, we must in the present exercise the maximum of power. The second theory is that some form of government has always existed in the past, exists now, and will continue to exist in the future; a society without a government is a sheer impossibility. Therefore society must be so ordered as to ensure the welfare of all. There may be certain amount of decentralisation, but all important matters must be under the centre. The third is our own theory. We too believe in a stateless society as our ultimate goal. We recognise that in the preliminary stages a certain measure of government is necessary, but we do not agree that it will continue to be necessary at a later stage. Neither do we agree that totalitarian dictatorship is necessary to ensure progress towards a stateless society. On the contrary we propose to proceed by decentralising administration and authority. In the final stage there would be no coercion but a purely moral authority, said Vinoba.

Government is not something natural, it is man-made. But the condition today is such that the moment one is born, he comes under the control of a government. The chief cause of all the turmoil and unrest found in the world is the managerial class. Some managers are rulers, some are officers, some are policemen and soldiers, and some are lawyers and judges. Thus they are of different types. There are some religious managers known as priests. The world is in disorder because of these managers. The people are like a well, while the government is like a bucket. In other words, the power of the people is greater.

'Power Politics' is one thing and 'strength politics' another. Some people run after power politics, but power results in the erosion of strength. Strength is increased by selfless service. Political power does not confer the strength needed to increase our social welfare. That strength and that spirit can only be found in those who serve society with single-minded devotion, untrammelled by bonds or by the duties of any office. Therefore, there should be within a society a large group continually engaged in service and continually on the alert. It should have experience in public affairs, but it should hold no position of authority and it should express itself fearlessly and dispassionately on public issues, so as to exert a moral influence both on the government and on the people. Such a group can be effective only if it keeps clear of office, not contemptuously but with in understanding of the limitation of power and with the realisation that the source of strength lies not in power but in the service of the community.

For hundreds of years there had been foreign rule. The people were made inactive. Everything is done by government servants. A mentality has developed that we have to do nothing. We want the same thing to continue after independence. It is termed 'freedom' when we are completely slaves. There is inactivity in the nature of India. We have to remove it and then work. Only then India will progress. At present entering politics only means lack of involvement in the service of the people. Involvement in politics implies involvement in jealousy, hatred, quarrels and in attempts to serve one's own interests. Nothing is being done for the good of others. In a country like India where there are innumerable differences like those of language, religion, caste, etc. politics will only create further differences. Hence there can be no progress in India without ending politics and establishing *lokniti,* politics of the people. Vinoba wants to say that this is an age of science. In this age politics has been left with no strength now. Man has acquired new types of weapons. Hence, if divisive politics will prosper, man is sure to be annihilated.

A real democracy means that every citizen is responsible for the welfare of society, and that every citizen's talents are being developed and used. Real democracy must rest itself not on force of arms but on the power of *ahimsa* and the organised good will of the people. That is the democracy we are striving for. The difference between democracy and other politics is that democrats do not believe in army. In their philosophy army has a secondary place. However, the recognition given to the army in practice though not wishing it in theory, converts democracy into military rule. Hence it should only be based on non-violence.

Our modern democracy came into being as a protest against the power of kings, and for that reason it suffers from the same faults as the monarchy it displaced — the real power remains in the hands of central government. Democracy is like a dairy milk, while monarchy is like a single cow's milk. A democratic government is representative of the sum total of its people's development. Mere counting of heads and elections are not the essence of democracy. At present we are talking about democracy and at the same time keeping capitalist economy and a military regime. We give lip-service to democracy but our actions are anti-democratic. That is why our democracy bears so little fruit and may soon bear none at all. The present democracy is a slave of bureaucracy.

It is no use saying that in a democracy people have the right and the opportunity to change the government every five years. A little serious thought will show how hollow this contention. Four or five years are not a small period in these days when scientific advance has changed all the old values of time and space. What one government does today in the five years of its tenure very often binds the successive governments also, and cannot be undone or left unfinished by them. Democracy and military rule are very close. For democracy claims to work for the welfare of society through representatives. Society is not asked to work for its own welfare. Everyone assures that you elect our party and we would set everything right, make society happy and abolish disparities. But when they are unable to fulfil their promises, people get dissatisfied. At the same time, they also feel oppressed by the laws. Under such conditions it becomes easy for the army to assume power, assuring the people of comforts and ease.

The democracy adopted in our country is a senseless imitation of the West. Here conditions are not like those prevalent there. Hence a lot of problems, troubles and obstacles have arisen. So long as we do not evolve and adopt a democracy that suits the conditions of our country, our troubles will not end. We shall have to seek measures that avoid conflicts and differences within the country. In India a democratic set-up has to be built up, consistent with the peculiar conditions and circumstances of the country. We have forgotten major languages and an equal number of States. The country is a vast one, about five times in area and six to seven times in population compared to England. In our country we have a number of religions with rich and philosophical backgrounds. The difference is easily perceptible, and yet we try to fully imitate England. Therefore, Vinoba wants to lay emphasis on two points. First, in elections the individual rather than the party should be given preference. Elections to Gram Panchayats, municipal boards etc. should be free of party lines. Members of the Lok Sabha should be regarded not as representatives of parties but of the whole country. Secondly, he wants the formation of an association or society which should be absolutely immune to party bickerings and affiliations. Such an association would have equal consideration for all parties and serve them equally. It will work as a lubricant to prevent clashes between them. If these two conditions are fulfilled, he believes we shall achieve some success in democracy in India.

Lokniti replaces the word *rajniti*. Though the word is new, the idea is an old one. It means that the authority should be that of love and it should be exercised from within. There should be no external authority. *Lokniti* means that power must actually pass into the hands of the people at all levels. Government must continuously either recede into background or wither away, and its place must be taken up by the people themselves. Initiative must pass to the people. After independence, the people have become less independent, less self-restraint. We have to rely on the government for everything. Things have come to such a pass that we expect the government to do everything while we do nothing, not only in social and religious matter like untouchability, but even in our domestic affairs. A law may solve our problem but it will not make us stronger. What people really need is to become aware of their own inner strength, and that they can only do if they solve some of their problems for themselves.

Today, in the name of the 'Welfare state', we are concentrating all power at the centre. Even if the people do get a certain amount of benefit out of it, Vinoba would still call it not 'well-fare' but 'ill-fare', because it keeps power in the hands of a few. The idea of non-violence will spread only when power is shared among the villagers.

Decentralisation is not to be confined merely to industries. The process of decentralisation applies equally fruitfully to the authority of the State. Even thinkers who are avowedly intent on building up a non-violent social order at times lose sight of this fact. They support the demand for industrial decentralisation, but at the sametime they often plead for a strong central authority for the preservation of the former. Vinoba submits that real freedom and peace can come only when people have established *Swaraj* or self-rule in small areas. Government will then be like a thread that keeps such self-sufficient and autonomous taluka units together. This is the only way of establishing peace in the world.

We want every village to have *Swaraj* — to manage its own affairs. We want to see all powers vested in the village, so that the job of the State Government will not be to give orders to the village, but instead to keep the villages in touch with one another. In the same way the Government in Delhi would have no authority over the States, but would maintain contact between them. The higher the level of Government, the more extensive would the liaison work become, and the more limited would be its direct authority. The direct authority, the material power, will be exercised by the villages. The Centre will be manned by persons of character and integrity who will thus exercise a moral authority. God practises this decentralisation. He has given all his creatures a share of intelligence in the scorpion and the snake, to the tiger and the man. It is true that the shares are unequal, but each one has some and God has decreed that each one should direct its life by its own intelligence. As a result the world has got on so well that God has been able to take a holiday, and men have even begun to doubt his existence.

We have fought against casteism and the practice of untouchability. Our fight against these evils is still going on. But a new division and casteism is becoming respectable. There are so many political parties. They grow like mushrooms and continue to sow seeds of division. Their function is to emphasize differences. A division of society among political warring groups is considered necessary for the growth of democracy. This artificial division in watertight separate parties has the sanction of political science. We have borrowed the apparatus, forms and institutions of democratic practice from the West. We have never cared to find out if they suited our ethos. The time has come when we have to re-examine and reassess the actual utility or value of some of the forms which we have adopted and are practising as a democratic ritual.

Where party politics are in vogue, one party holds all the power and another has none. The second is always contending with the first to get the power for itself. The party in power boasts to the people about its own great qualities and achievements; the opposition points out its shortcomings and mistakes. Every party speaks ill of the other parties; this absorption in fault-finding is the result of their worship of power. They all dance attendance on power, and worship at its alter, and there is a continual tug-of-war between them. Each party claims that if you return it to power, it will lead you to heaven, but that if you return the other fellows to power, they will lead you into hell. No one tells you the real truth — that your destiny, heaven or hell, is in your hands, and that no one but yourself can take you there. As long as this sort of thing goes on, there will be no contentment, no peace and no freedom in the world. People are fed up with parties, which imply wasting of strength. One party weakens another party, and then this weakens the first one too. They both together weaken the country.

Political parties, whether in our country or outside, which subscribe to narrow ideals and loyalties, are out-of-date in this Age of Science. They are the remnants of an age which is fast disappearing. We have to understand that party politics is so narrow and useless a thing that it makes no sense today. The ill-will and jealousies that were confined in old times to a few feudal chiefs or kings, have now been made country wide by party politics. A party can come into existence only when there be an obsence of right thinking.

It is the duty of Sarvodaya workers to stand between the rulers and the ruled, to point out mistakes on both sides, to foster mutual trust and understandings, and to increase the people's strength. They should identify themselves neither with the government nor with the people. They should be independent of both, and render true service to both, by pointing out the virtues and faults of both sides; they should be friends of all but be members of no party.

The majority method (of taking decisions) has come from the West and the Westerners consider it to be a progressive political idea. To us it appears to be a totally crude one. Perceiving truth has nothing to do with numerical majority. Formerly decisions were enforced on the point of sword; now-a-days they are enforced by a majority instead. We claim that we have given up the use of sword because it is an unintelligent way of doing things. But majority rule is not an intelligent way either. Matters cannot be rightly settled by counting heads; the only result is discontent and strife, and everyone is geared to the effort to overthrow one's opponent. At one time the minority ruled over the majority. It did not result in any good. As a reaction to it, emerged the rule of the majority over the minority. It is no pure love, but love born as a reaction. It has led to tensions in the world and given rise to the new problem of majority and minority everywhere.

Things will go rightly only when we accept the idea of unanimity. The Indian idea of a village Panchayat holds a special place among the political ideas of the world. It included the principle of 'God speaks through the five,' which was accepted throughout India. This means that five members of the Panchayat must reach a common mind, and then only the decision was made. But now we 'pass' a decision by a majority of four to one or three to two, as though God speaks in the three'. Vinoba contends that such proposals are not really passed, so long as they fail to convince even one person. Only that proposal deserves to 'pass' which commends itself to all. We must revive this ancient Indian tradition, for a people's democracy can only be built on mutual trust and cooperation. Truth and cooperation are essential to the prospering of its affairs. Without them, neither in India nor in the world can non-violence ever be maintained.

The increase of communal differences is the first evil consequence of elections. A second is that in the present set-up it is not possible for a man to stand for election unless he has wealth or property. We hold elections, but we do not even know our candidates by sight. Hundreds of thousands of people cast their votes, but so far from knowing the character of the man they vote for, they do not even know his face. For the sake of elections we spend our money, we allow the poison of communalism to spread, and in the end we have no guarantee that those elected will be worthy of our trust. The election has its own ethics. Its three principles are self-praise, speaking ill of others, and telling lies.

At least the present system of direct elections should be changed into that of indirect elections. For it, the party differences must be eliminated from the villages. There should be a general body consisting of all over 21 and it should elect an executive by unanimity. Unanimity and non-party village organisation are essential conditions for it. The higher bodies should be elected by Gram Sabhas, the village assemblies. Thus the elections should be indirect.

Whenever there are elections, no candidate of any party should be elected blindly. It is not right to elect an undeserving person simply because he belongs to one's own party. Elections do have some significance in the history of the country. But Vinoba wants to say that we have attached too much importance to politics. He does not say this about India only. He says it about the whole world. There would be no peace in the world as long as it gives that much importance to politics as it has given so far.

Sarvodaya does not mean good government or majority rule, it means freedom from government, it means decentralisation of power. We want to do away with government by politicians and replace it by a government of the people, based on love, compassion and equality. Decisions should be taken, not by majority, but by unanimous consent; and they should be carried out by the united strength of the ordinary people of the village.

Gram Panchayat is India's unique contribution to social thinking. In remote past when Europe had hardly awakened to social consciousness, we in India had made considerable progress in political and social thinking. The Panchayat system was evolved for dealing justice to all and providing protection and education to all. All had to submit to the unanimously agreed decisions of these councils. It can be regarded as a decentralised social order.

The chief features of Gram Swaraj are — (1) Disputes of the village will not be decided outside (2) The village will defend itself by its own strength (3) It will control its imports and exports (4) It will produce its own food. Village affairs would be managed by common consent, and not on any party basis. There would be a General Assembly of all villagers above the age of twenty-one. They would chose an executive committee of five, or seven, or ten members, which would run the administration of the village. But its decision would have to be unanimous. We have to make every village a complete and a thorough State in miniature. Thus, in every village there would be all the various departments as they are now in a State, such as health, industries, agriculture, education, justice, etc. As there is a Foreign Affairs Department with respect to the relations with other countries, there will be in every village a special department which would handle the affairs pertaining to other villages.

The role of the Centre in a Gram Swaraj polity are the following (1) The Central Government will be a link to keep the village republic together. (2) It will manage the railway, postal and such other services. (3) It will look after big industries and mines. (4) It will be in charge of defence and external relations of the country. (5) It will be an overall advisory body. Powers will remain with the constituent republics. The Central authority will gradually assume the shape of an advisory council.

Vinoba had given the programme for Gram Panchayats. He said, "Every Panchayats should organise a study circle which will acquaint the people of the village with new ideas and important developments taking place in the national and international fields. The centre will specially provide for the study of Gandhian and *Sarvodya literature.* Selected writings from such literature should be read out and explained to the people. The Panchayats should undertake to bring about an increase in production as one of their primary responsibilities. As long as the produce does not increase and the vast unemployment found in the villages is not liquidated, villagers are not likely to feel the urge for offering their cooperation to any developmental authority. The Panchayat should consider it their duty to see that no person within their areas remains unemployed and goes hungry. Just as the boycott of foreign goods helped the attainment of *Swaraj,* so would the boycott of mill cloth help bring about Gramraj. Since land is the basic factor of all production, the land must be distributed to all. The ownership of land should belong to the village and there should be no one without land. The real power of the Panchayats lies in the people's support. The Panchayats should therefore follow their will and act under their control. They should not care whether the Government recognises them or not. The people must always rely on their own strength and go forward. The panchayats should carry out these five functions. Then only it will be possible to establish Ramrajya in our villages".[7]

Isolation and separation, in the world today, means annihilation and death. Co-existence has become a condition for survival. Non-violence and brotherhood are no mere altruistic and idealistic concepts. They have the sanction of stark realism. Because of the phenomenal growth of science, brotherhood and love have acquired a new relevance. Society cannot last without them. If hate and rivalry continue as before, human society will be destroyed by modern science. If brotherhood and love become the cementing force in society, modern science will create a new world of freedom, peace and plenty.

The objective of Sarvodaya is to demolish the walls standing between various countries. Just as we are today free to move within India from one State to another, are welcome to live anywhere, can go for sight-seeing, education or business, similarly a man should be free to come and go to any place in the world. This is what we have to do. According to the non-violent way of thinking, human society is one, and in it separate nations are conceived of merely for the sake of convenience. If a particular nation has the good sense to adopt non-violence, it will not regard itself as separate from and as opposed to the others. It will be as anxious to safeguard the legitimate interests of neighbouring nations as those of its own.

Merely an absence of war is not peace. What is needed for peace is a constructive approach. These days absence of war is regarded as peace. But peace really connotes absence of fear. There would be peace only when no part of the world is afraid of or exploited by any other part. By peace Vinoba means something dynamic, something which will develop the power of the individual and the dynamic strength of the people to a degree that will enable them to meet any situation. Shanti or peace, therefore, cannot be negative. It has to be something positive.

Peace as wrongly understood in India is not peace but lack of sensitivity. What peace is there in lying calmly on a cushion bed. Peace has value when there are problems and efforts are being made to solve them. If peace means maintenance of status quo, that peace is worthless. Peace is something mental or spiritual. If there be peace in our life, it will affect the whole world.

Some advocates of peace point out that many nations of the world require peace today for they cannot develop themselves without it. Hence they desire peace in the world. Their movement is known as the World Peace Movement. There are several European countries which desire peace in spite of the communists being very strong there. As long as mankind had no independent thirst for peace, there can be no peace in the world. Another endeavour is also going on for the establishment of peace in the world. It is of the Moral Rearmament for which some people are collectively working. They try to go to other countries and to do something noble so that there be greater mutual love and friendliness. Non-violent resistance to war is the final result of a non-violent attitude and not the first as many western pacifists seem to think.

It is wrong to think that a country's strength lies in its military power. A nation will become really strong only if it is free from internal conflicts, if it becomes self-sufficient and the people within are united by bonds of love. If we make our country strong like this, whatever be the threats or dangers that may confront us, none of them will cast any shadow on us. On the other hand, our greatness will certainly have a good influence on outside world. This country will have to be defended not by arms but by fearlessness, ethical behaviour and unity.

Nuclear weapons should, of course, be abolished. But the conventional weapons appear to be no less frightening. The nuclear arms tend to bring us nearer to non-violence because they impel man to think and ponder. But pistols and daggers put non-violence far away. These weapons appear to be small, but they are the parents of nuclear arms. Renunciation of arms can take place only when there will be a plan for decentralised production. It cannot happen earlier. *Sarvodya* thought is worthless if the Sarvodayees feel that army is indispensable. It will be an act of wisdom as well as courage if India reduces her armament. This act will enhance her reputation and prestige in the world. It will make her powerful in the real sense.

We should create such conditions in the country that the police or the army becomes unnecessary for internal peace. If we can achieve this, the next step of the extension of non-violence to external defence, would become apparent. For peace and security within the country, we must cast off mutual differences and share our weal and woe together. Sharing decreases misery and increases joy.

Vinoba does not believe in dividing men as criminals and non-criminals. To him, no man is a criminal. Some men are branded as such and are put in jail. But some criminals are to be found outside-only they are not so in the eyes of law. It is held that the pleader, the judge and the police, etc. work to eradicate crimes and robberies. But they are all of the same fraternity as thieves and robbers. They punish the innocent and feed the culprit.

People are afraid that crime will increase if a deterrent like capital punishment is abolished. Those who know something of the psychology of a criminal will understand that a deterrent like capital punishment hardly enters his mind when he is seized by some insane passion. Our civilisation and culture have looked upon public opinion as the final sanction of right social behaviour. It is not the penal code that keeps men and women on the right path. The existence of proper values and public opinion is an effective guide to good conduct. In an ideal Sarvodaya society law will not need a penal code. It will express itself as the conscience of the people.

There are always in society a few noble individual, who do not require public opinion to hold them within the limits of morality. Similarly there are also wayward and indiscriminate individuals who, unmindful of a public opinion, go against the laws of morality. But the general public or the great majority of people observe what is ordained and avoid what is prohibited by public opinion. Such public opinion naturally constitutes the basis of law or restraint, and the vast majority of people always respect it. The few wayward individuals who remain outside this number should be put in the company of the few who are highsouled, instead of being submitted to forcible restraint. It is obvious that if we are really anxious to eradicate crime, then we must find out its root cause which lies in the faulty organisation of society. We must purify and where necessary rebuild the social organisation. Efforts should be made to introduce and establish in our social consciousness the idea that it is a sin to hoard wealth and avoid physical labour. Love, compassion, generosity and forgiveness have a higher place in life as moral attributes then hard-hearted punishment.

The basic problem of the world today is the establishment of peace. Perhaps in no other age has there been such a world-hunger for peace. Today there is an explosive situation in the country. There can be a sudden explosion for any reason whatsoever. The *shanti sena* is not a new proposal. We owe both the word and the idea behind it to Gandhiji, who himself endeavoured to give it a practical shape. He was both its commander and its first soldier.

The *shanti sena* is an army which offers its services in perpetuity to all men without distinction. To be a *shanti sainik* means to be prepared to leave everything, home, public work, etc. and go wherever he may be called. This is one point in which he differs from other *lok sevaks;* his other pledges are the same. The work of the *shanti sainik* has therefore two aspects: his regular day-to-day duties are of a 'Seva Sainik' while his occasional duties are those of the *shanti sainik.* It is not the duty of the *shanti sainik* to find solutions for all problems of society. His job is to help people in their physical troubles, and do his best to help them also in their mental worries. In addition, he will be taking every chance of helping them to understand the ideas of *Bhoodan, Gramdan* etc. and bringing *Sarvodaya* literature to their notice.

Those who enlist in the *shanti sena* will consider it their duty to serve the whole community, to help all the needy, without regard for caste, religion, sect, party or any other distinction. The *shanti sainik* must treat everyone, high or low in the same way; like water he must be humble, gentle, clean, pure and cool. The first requirement for a *shanti sainik* is that no one should be afraid of him. The various political parties also must have no fear of him; if they are afraid, he must show by his conduct that he has no partisan spirit, that he is out to serve without looking for any reward, and that he has no inclination to join any party but is working only for *sarvodaya,* the welfare of all, and is ready to give his life, if need arise, in that cause.

A member of *shanti sena*, whether a man or woman, must have a living faith in non-violence. This is only possible if one has a living faith in God. This messenger of peace should have equal respect for all the prominent religions of the world. He should have the knowledge of the principles common to various religions. The *shanti sainik* accepts the principle of *aparigraha*, non-possession, and does not accumulate unnecessary possessions. But this does not mean that he must give up all he has.

The main principle of *shanti sena* is that they should be free from partisanship, free from hatred, free from fear. They will trust one another, will fear none, and will frighten none. They will consider no man their enemy; their hearts will be filled with love. This is the pledge of the *shanti sainik*.

It is necessary that *shanti sainiks* are trained for their work. Some portions of the primary training of the army is also essential. It is about discipline, drill, chorus singing, etc. A volunteer should know how to remove the wounded. He should have such articles with him, as are needed for First Aid. He should know how to extinguish fire, how to enter safely a place on fire, how to climb up with or without a load and to descend safely. For increase of knowledge, refresl.er courses should also be arranged. They should teach the worker how he can serve best. The members should have a special dress so that they may be identified without any difficulty.

If women will take up the work of *shanti sena,* the face of the world will change, and we shall be able to achieve freedom from the problems which we are facing today in the country and abroad. In this age of science, when men's brains have become paralysed, if our women come forward with their divine qualities of restraint and modesty, and use their mother-power, they can establish the rule of compassion. In the path of violence, men will always lead. But in the path of non-violence women can go ahead of them. So it is essential that women should lead, and that too in their own way.

REFERENCES

1. *Young India*, 19.3.31.
2. *Harijan*, 28.7.46.
3. *Young India*, 25.8.31.
4. M.K. Gandhi, *My Experiments with Truth*. p. 369.
5. *Harijan*, 11.2.39.
6. *Ibid.*, 28.9.47.
7. *Ibid.*, 11.9.54.

7

EDUCATIONAL THOUGHT OF GANDHI AND VINOBA

Any investment in education is a worthy contribution and can be considered as an asset for the country for the present and for the years to come. In a country like India education holds the premier position in the social life of the people and their development. The nature and quality of our future generation will be remarkable depending upon the quality and curriculam of the education and the methodology adopted for its imparting. Unfortunately we are continuing our experiments, too far and too fast in the field of education, without taking heed of the effects or potential results of one or the other experiments undertaken. Many a time the content of education is divorced from reality of life and the values and major elements in social life get diluted in the process.

Gandhiji was not an academician nor an educationist in the rigid sense of the term. But his views on education has embossed a serious and lasting outlook towards education that could be of high value to Indian education system at all time. His contribution in this regard could be considered as most important one to India for her social development. He had a broad outlook towards life as such and education in particular. To him, education means an all-round drawing out of the best in child and man-body, mind and spirit. It is one of the means whereby man and woman can be educated. Literacy in itself is no education. It shows that he was viewing education as a means for all-round human development.

Gandhiji remarked that the optimum enrichment and development of personality should be achieved through education. As a social philosopher, he wanted education to be a powerful medium for social change and development. He was of the firm view that unless the individual change takes place the social development is impossible. So, he gave importance to character building and reshaping of the attitudes and values. Literacy education is of no value if it is not able to build up a sound character. He stressed for a free and self-supporting education. He kept the ideal of achieving self-realisation as the ultimate aim of education.

To quote Gandhiji, "Man is neither mere intellect, nor the gross animal body, nor the heart, nor soul alone. A proper and harmonious combination of all the three is required for the making of the whole man and constitutes the true economics of education".[1] True education is that which draws out and stimulates the spiritual, intellectual and physical faculties of the children. He wanted to base education on indigenous culture because, otherwise, it would make the educated unfit for the service of the community and make them foreigners in their own land. He held the view that the social aim of education does not come in conflict with the individual aim. Man is to serve society and society is to help man. For the attainment of these aims, he had offered the Basic Education.

Gandhiji wanted to establish a *Sarvodaya* order of society in India. The gist of Basic Education could be presented as follows—Education should be made free and compulsory for the children in the age group of 7-14 years. Gandhiji wanted to make education self-supporting. That is why he emphasised on learning by doing and through the practice of bread labour. He said, "My *Nai Talim* is not dependent, should come from the educational process itself, whatever the criticism may be, I know that the only education is that which is self-supporting".[2] After the completion of seven years of free and compulsory education, the children should be capable of taking up some meaningful occupation enabling them to stand on their own foot. This will help the children develop confidence and security as well as making them realistic and productive.

Education, as Gandhiji visualised, was one which is craft-centred. In fact craft was considered as the medium for earning and development. He wanted education to revolve around a teacher and not books. He always felt that the true text-book for the pupil is his teacher, because children take in much more and with less labour through their ears than through their eyes. To him, the teacher was to be most respected and most spiritual man in society. He should act as the true model for the student. The type of education that he visualised was based on the tacit assumption of intimate interaction between the teacher and students. Values like cooperation, discipline, sacrifice, integrity, fearlessness, etc., are part of such teacher-student relationship. Basic education stressed very much on discipline and not in unlimited freedom. No training is possible without discipline and restriction.

The medium of instruction should be mother tongue. A foreign language deprives them of the spiritual and social heritage of the nation, and renders them to that extent unfit for the service of the country. The introduction of English language by the British people blocked the development of Indian languages. The foreigners had their own plan of exploitation in this regard. Mother tongue, being the most simple for any child, is the easiest one to pickup. The 'Higher Education' should not be costly one and it should not be at the expense of the poor tax payers. However, we could see that only the middle and upper classes are the main beneficiaries of the present education system sponsored out of the money contributed by the poor.

Gandhiji wanted to bridge the gap between rich and poor through the instrument of technology. He felt the need for integration of industry and education. He expected the technological advancement to facilitate the over-all development of the country. However, he cautioned the nation to limit the dependence on machines so that man may not become its slave. He aimed at developing a spiritual man dedicated to truth and non-violence. Education should always lead man closer to spiritual attainment and progress. Instead of moral education, he advocated the teaching of ethical ideas.

Gandhiji stressed the importance of non-violence to be attained through education. True education and violence are fundamentally opposed to each other and true education can be given through non-violence and this is the central idea of his education scheme. He held that students should not participate in politics. To maintain the sober and serene nature of education, the interweaving of politics in education could be a blockade. He maintained the view that politics will be a barrier to the development of students. It affects their concentration and leads to disgression from the studies. He was not against state interference. He wanted financial assistance from the state, but the state should not interfere in the educational activities. He was fully aware of the possible consequences such an intervention could lead to. So he was cautioning to keep the education free from various political interference so that it can maintain its purity and independence.

Gandhiji's concept of 'education' and '*swadeshi*' are inter-woven. Without *swadeshi*, there cannot be any meaningful national educational system. The problem of educated people seeking the first opportunity to work abroad, as seen today, is definitely a proof as to why Gandhiji cautioned and stressed the concept of *swadeshi* in the field of education. He laid much stress on the character formation. He adhered to the principle of simple living and high thinking to be adopted and achieved through education. A luxurious life spoils the mind, making it rigid while life based on voluntary poverty and simplicity is the one most desirable. He proved this through his life.

Gandhiji considered prayer as an important medium. As a votary of universal religion, he stressed the importance of prayer in all walks of life, particularly in education. He recommended prayer and reading or recitation of holy scriptures for inclusion in a programme of moral education. He was of the opinion that to face and deal with national problems like population, energy crisis and unemployment, the need of the hour is to make people realise the causes and consequences of these basic human problems. He was optimistic in the sense that meaningful and proper education can put effective check on such problems and thereby ensuring progress of the nation. He remarked that the students must be trained to think independently, critically and creatively. For this, he stressed on the three H's (Head, Heart and Hand) rather than three R's (Reading, Writing and Arithmetic).

It was Gandhiji who brought the Indian women into the arena of socio-political movements. Till then, women were kept dark within four walls. As a practical reformist, he was fully convinced of the need for women's education to liberate them fully from their chains. Though education was conceived of as a medium for acquiring knowledge and skills, he was against the educated youth waiting for government jobs or professional employment. The educated people should utilise their acquired skills and techniques for the development of the society in general and the villages in particular. Since he was very much aware of the fact that India's future lies in villages, the stress for education as a meaningful weapon for social development of the villages was suggested. Hence the role of educated people and their commitment to the cause of the poor citizens in the villages were considered highly significant.

To Gandhiji, a true education encompasses the entire vista of man's life and activities on earth. That was the reason why he dealt with the problems of education and experimented with it not merely within the mural limits of a school but in wider fields of human activites. It was the reason why he did not postulate or stick to a single aim of education or develop any definite thesis on its basis like others. He pointed out that the world produced great men long before schools and colleges came into existence. To him, the aim of education was individual in the sense that it ensures freedom or salvation of individual soul from all kinds of bondage —superstition, ignorance, egocentric impulses or narrowness of mind.

He explained that man has risen to his present status by learning to adjust his individualism to the requirements of social progress. The highest aim of education is to provide or create an ideal atmosphere of knowledge and truth so that the essential individuality of each person may bloom fully in conformity with the highest good of society.

According to some critics Gandhiji was a great champion of strict discipline in educational matters. His approach was essentially positive. But a deep study of Gandhiji unquestionably proves that he never preferred any 'unlimited freedom' or any kind of imposed restriction that usually stand against the natural growth of a child's body, mind and spirit. He insisted on different kinds of training and disciplines that help the students to grow from within. He upheld old *brahmacharya* ideals of self-control to be the key of all kinds of moral upliftment and success. He was against any kind of 'artificial restraint upon the students' all-round growth.

Gandhiji insisted that teachers should occupy a pivotal position in India's future educational system. Without systematic efforts to improve their quality, it would be impossible to make India's educational institutions more purposeful. It is for the teachers to mould the character of the young generation which is entrusted to their care, they are in a real sense, the great architects of a nation. They should take the task of teaching as an act of the performance of their *dharma* which was in the name of *yagna* or sacrificial act of worshipping God. He agrees that a child learns more through his senses and the primary business of a school should be to train children in cooperative and mutually helpful living by providing them maximum opportunity to use muscles, sight, feeling as well as hearing and by employment of energy, originality and initiative. But the novel feature of his philosophy consists in the fact that he did not mean to supplement literacy with manual training, but makes manual training the means of literacy and intellectual training.

Gandhiji believed that music should be included in the syllabus at school. He remarked that the modulation of the voice is as necessary as the training of the hand. To him, music meant rhythm, order and its effect is electrical, it immediately soothes. He emphasized that music should not be the prerogative of the few but must be nationalised in the modern sense. He believed that society itself is a school and its conscious and unconscious influences mould the mind and character of its people. Hence educational. institutions must make arrangements for moulding youth into patterns approved by her society. Accordingly, an ideal education should consist of an effort to know the country one lives in, in its geographical, historical and cultural perspective and compromising its highest ideas in the past and its potentials in the future. He believed that the educational system introduced by Lord Macaulay was very contrary to the spiritual heritage, economic interest, cultural integrity of Indian people as a whole.

Gandhiji believed that as an individual finds his fullest expression being a member of a society, a nation finds its fullest entity only by being a member of an international community. He believed that this adjustment of knowledge and accommodation of different views of different people is possible where there is a larger scope of enjoying a life of common living, knowing and understanding the religions, languages and cultures of other people. At the same time he warned his countrymen that while they should receive the best in every culture they should not be carried away, blindly, by the tide of any outside influences.

It is sad that Gandhian ideas on education was not properly understood and accepted in the very land that gave birth to him. Instead of making efforts to understand his ideology in the proper perspective, many were on the lookout for finding the loopholes in the scheme. In their efforts to find the errors, out of their own ignorance and lack of positive outlook, they missed the gist and true content of the scheme. Such a critical look towards his plan of education was definitely hampering and unfortunate. The critics lacked the optimistic and conservative outlook towards achieving an ideal society as he desired to bring in. Education, as he perceived, was a continuous and life-long process. It starts from the conception and ends with death. He had taken a broad view of education thereby freeing it from the clutches of specified institutions and throwing it open for the common man for his entire life.

II

Education does not call anything new into being, but it is the means by which the sleeping essence is awakend. It implies making oneself fit for society. By it is meant the development of the powers of the intellect, the sense organs and the physical body, and this can be had by association with noble souls. Self-control, fearlessness and independence of thinking, these are the three tests of education. Only that country is educated wherein these three qualities find expression. Education should be looked at from two viewpoints — that of spiritual life and that of the situation around. The two tests of education are that it should lead to spiritual development and should correspond to the situation.

Education is a by-product of practical work. A man who follows any useful occupation is being educated by it, whether he knows it or not.

Children ought to be educated in the same way. Adults learn the hard way by their mistakes. Learning for the pupil must be an unconscious, natural process. There are two things which ought to be looked for from education. The first is that education, which is given at the national expense, ought to be of use in practical affairs. A child should be so educated that he is competent to come forward and serve the world around him, and return tenfold whatever he has received. The second thing which we expect from education is that all the student's faculties should develop as a harmonious, integrated whole.

There is no true joy for the man whose life is cut off from the heavens above and the world of nature around. This means that the task before education is to change the whole system of values and the way of life that is current in our cities. At present mistakes are being made in the field of education, in two ways. First, millions of people do not get education, and, secondly, those who get it, do not receive the right type of education. Thus the condition is that on one side there is lack of education and, on the other miseducation.

The present education is concerned only with two faculties—power of memory and capacity for arguments. There are several other faculties more important than these, but the present education pays no attention towards their development. Considering the needs of the country, this education is of no use. The state of affairs is that a boy starting from the age of six, continues to study till the age of twenty or twenty-one, and for these fifteen years he does no work or labour. He is incapable of standing inclemencies of weather and of doing anything, be it agriculture, carpentry, weaving or cooking. He has no knowledge of dietetic. Thus he comes out of the school without any preparation for practical living.

One great misfortune that befell this country on account of the British rule was that while some got English education, others did not get it, creating two classes, one of the learned and the other of the unlearned. This further led to an increase of differences and conflicts. The second misfortune was that the standard of living of those who were given education was raised, which was against the cultural traditions of this country. The third misfortune was that work was not linked with education. The result is the tendency in the educated to enjoy pleasures without doing work and to look down upon physical labour. These three defects of education are as dangerous as the derangement of the three humours of the body under the Indian system of medicine, which proves fatal to a patient.

Students are not imparted such education which will inspire them to help increase production and to make physical labour entertaining. Rather, they are imparted education which makes them good for nothing. Hence Vinoba detects seeds of danger and ill omen in the prevailing system of education. If it persists for some more time, it will destroy villages and drag the whole country into the ditch of urbanisation. A complaint is made these days that students lack discipline, but it is so because they have no respect for teachers, and this respect is absent because there are no real teachers these days. They are simply employees imparting education.

Vinoba held that just as judiciary is independent and the government has no authority over it, similarly the education department should be free and independent. If the education is in the hands of the government, it is open to two objections: (i) It acquires a rigid form and is coloured by the complexion of the government. (ii) All teachers become employees. What should really be is that education should be in the hands of public men of knowledge and if the government so desires it may somewhat help it. The education of each village should be in the hands of that village itself. Of course, the government may run such colleges and schools of technology and science as are free of any ideology, but with regard to the education involving development of mind and heart, the whole of it should be in the hands of the people themselves.

Most of our people live in villages, the education of the nation as a whole should be village-centred, so that the villages may benefit by it. The people of the towns must be given the kind of education which will direct their interest towards the villages, so that there may be healthy cooperation between the town and the village. The country will greatly suffer if the towns get one kind of education and the villages get of another kind, incompatible with it. 'Today when we want to rebuild our country, we ought to see that the education of our boys and girls consists of both learning and self-control. The learning would include control over the senses and proficiency in *karmayoga*. A student must be proficient in agriculture, cow-keeping, spinning and weaving, and a few other useful crafts. He should be good at all things which are helpful and necessary for village life. He must have acquired the capacity to earn his living in an independent way so that there never will be any occasion for him to feel driven to seek employment and thus suffer loss of freedom. If he has learnt to control his senses, serves his teachers and do his work efficiently and devotedly, he may be regarded as having mastered the self-control. Then he must also acquire knowledge; knowledge of the body for health, knowledge of the self for spiritual development and knowledge of the language for social intercourse. The knowledge of these things will enable him to do his *dharma*, that is, to do his duty towards himself and towards the society of which he is a part'.[3]

Nai Talim is a philosophy of living, it is an attitude towards life that we have to bring to all our work. That education which destroys old values and establishes new values, will be called *Nai Talim*. *Nai Talim* is not a system, it is a far-reaching educational idea. It is a seed-thought like the *Brahma-Vichar* which was so widespread in India and to which so many different systems of thought were all rooted.

There are several purposes of imparting education through crafts. The greatest of them is to remove the vanity of the educated and to link action to knowledge. The purpose of *Nai Talim* will not be served by teaching students a little of some craft. Boys and girls receiving their education through *Nai Talim* will be so proficient in their crafts that they will perform their work as easily and naturally as fish swim in water. *Nai Talim* is in complete opposition to the prevailing socio-economic system. If it is said that Basic Education is but one method of teaching whereby children are taught various subjects through the medium of handwork, it is entirely a mistake. *Nai Talim* or Basic Education cannot but create a new social order. It cannot live unless it did so. Some people think that *Nai Talim* and ordinary schools is that latter's knowledge is superficial while former's is solid and firmly grounded. This is because their instruction tends to be theoretical while ours springs from experience, so that ours has an assurance which their lacks.

The principle of *Nai Talim* is that knowledge and work are both forms of the same thing and therefore it is impossible to distinguish between knowledge-process and work-process. Educational activities are those which from one point of view appear to be learning, while from another angle they appear to be labour. There is no real educational activity when the knowledge-process is isolated, nor is there any education in the labour-process alone. A real educational activity is one where we cannot tell which of the two predominates. Moreover, this integration must be natural and unimposed.

The philosophy of *Nai Talim* does not accept the unequal values assigned by our present society to physical and mental work. It takes the position that every kind of service rendered by a man, whether it is physical or mental, is ethical in its nature; the salary which is given to him is economic in its nature. The value of an ethical act cannot be calculated in economic terms. The spiritual principle of *Nai Talim* is that knowledge and work are not two things but one. It is a mistake to say that knowledge is higher than work or work higher than knowledge. *Nai Talim* education is based on the unity of knowledge and work. Knowledge is gained in the most natural way, for whatever we do becomes a channel of learning. The social principle of *Nai Talim* is that all human lives are equally to be respected. All the various social and class divisions are therefore forms of falsehood.

Education prior to that of the university will be for self-reliance, and the education of the university will be through self-reliance. Self-sufficiency in *Nai Talim* has three meanings. The first is that one should not depend upon others for one's daily bread. The second is that one should have developed the power to acquire knowledge by oneself. The third is that a man should be able to rule over oneself, to control his senses and his thoughts.

Nai Talim need not have the same form everywhere. There may be several of them. We should choose such a craft as touches every aspect of life. The earlier *Nai Talim* has become old now. At that time the only basic craft was that of spinning. The new teachers will have new means to convey knowledge. It is to be understood that the vehicles of knowledge used several years earlier will not do now. Hence in this age the old teaching tools will not do. It is true that even small tools are useful for teaching children, but they will have new implements after a year or two, and they will be taught through them. It seems to be considered as a must that all social studies be taught only through crafts. But this rigidity of outlook is mistaken.

There is no need to go on teaching from cradle to the grave. Give the knowledge that is needed today; see that your students becomes capable of learning for himself whatever he may need in future; call into play his own latent powers. There are no rules and regulations about what items of knowledge should be included in a *Nai Talim* syllabus, and what should not be included. All kinds of knowledge may come in, but on one condition— a condition that challenges us. The child should be given the knowledge that is needed to satisfy the demands of his life today. If we reckon our syllabus by subjects, there will be no end to it, and no value. *Nai Talim* must provide complete knowledge of all that is basic in life. There is no need to memorise great chunks of history or meaningless lists of kings. But they must know the fundamental ideas by which man lives and grows. Some knowledge of philosophy, religion and ethics is essential. The children must know the basic concepts of science. They must be thoroughly familiar with the laws of health, nutrition, hygiene, cookery, etc. *Nai Talim* must demand thoroughness in these fields of knowledge, and also a thorough mastery of language, the ability to express one's ideas in the proper way.

The mother tongue and the national language constitute our two eyes. One who knows only one of them, will be considered one-eyed. The Sanskrit language is the third eye. We require the knowledge of the mother tongue to sense the people, the knowledge of Hindi for fostering nationalism and that of Sanskrit for religion and philosophy. The English language is highly developed. There are priceless treasures in it, and therefore if someone wants to learn it, he must. But there is a scientific way of learning a language. First of all, the mother tongue would be fully learnt with its grammar, and then one can learn any other language also easily. Many people consider education to be incomplete without English.

No irrelevant knowledge be given; only that knowledge be imparted which has a bearing on life. The second thing to be kept in mind is that we should not think about the various subjects in isolation. The child should not feel at the time of learning that it is being taught arithmetic or history or literature. Knowledge is one whole, it cannot be divided.

The medium of education should be the regional language of the State. Roughly speaking, Vinoba said that it should be the mother tongue. The national language should be a compulsory subject for all from the beginning to the end. In order that the services of university teachers be available throughout India, no matter to what particular regions they belong to, they should have the option of lecturing in the national language, if they are unable to do so in the regional language.

Religious teaching is a subject of great interest and importance. Vinoba held that true religious teaching is not a matter of literature. The essence of religion is a sound character, faith in God, and the conviction that the soul is other than the body. This essential religion can only be learnt from the company of good men. His plan for religious teaching is to choose good persons as teachers. Art has a place in school syllabus from the very first class, for without it we cannot realise the ideal of education through craft. Books do most certainly have a place in education as tools of knowledge but it is a very minor place. The major need for the teacher and the student is to become work-partners, and this can happen only when the distinction between the teacher, teaching and the student learning can be overcome. We never seem to have any doubt that by reading a boy or a girl is obtaining knowledge, and that reading is in fact the direct road to knowledge. It is nothing of the sort; on the contrary, book learning is like a curtain that shuts off from the world of real things.

Today our education is robbing a child of all initiative and inculcates fear in him. If he commits a mistake, he is beaten. So out of fear he becomes obedient. That is, instead of imparting fearlessness, you have taught him cowardice. If there is indiscipline among students, the fault lies with the teachers, the educational system and the social order. Today discipline has been made a virtue to be acquired and observed in preference to all others. Vinoba said that in fact the teacher should feel remorse if his students accepts his teachings without being really convinced. He should be happy if a student rejects his teachings and thinks independently for himself.

Adult education should be through craftsmanship, so as to enable the unemployed to do useful work and at the same time to develop their intelligence. Vinoba held that full provision for education ought to be made in every village. Each one of them should have its university or *vidyapeeth.* For, every village, no matter how small, is a microcosm; it contains the whole world in miniature. Therefore, complete education must be available there. The village is in close touch with the natural world of creation, and therefore has ready at hand the materials for the study of physical and natural sciences. The human community is established in the villages from ancient times; history and sociology can well be studied there. Moreover, the greater intimacy in which men live in villages is conducive to the development of ethics and religion.

The teachers and the students will be provided with a well equipped library necessary for them. They will be supplied with the tools and instruments required by them. They will have the needed land and other things. Some buildings too will be constructed for them. The rest they will build for themselves. Having done all this for them they would be told not to expect more. Thereafter let them live collectively and present before the country a model of the best type of life. There will be discussions, there will be experiments, and the results of these experiments will be placed before the country. But the main feature of this university will be that both the students and the teachers will stand on their own legs, work with their hands and earn their living. And that too not just anyhow, but in the very best manner.

When we take an examination, a supervisor has to be appointed to watch us, to see that no student copies from another. It is a very saddening spectacle. For if it is possible to suspect us of being capable of copying from others, then, as students, we have already failed. This test of education is completely one-sided. What it does at the utmost is to examine the ability for the argumentation and the power of memory. It cannot find out the progress made by the boy in what we term 'self-development'.

Government jobs should not be linked with the university degrees.

Every department should conduct its own examination in which anyone can appear. On being successful in them, one is to be considered qualified for the job. This would provide encouragement to private educational institutions and at many places educational experiments would be tried.

Men and women generally need the same qualities. Such qualities as love, parental affection, devotion, etc., should equally develop in men and women. Some think that the knowledge of cookery is for women only. Vinoba considers it to be incorrect. Both should have it. However, there may be some difference. Women can learn a few things particularly. They can develop art to a greater extent, but in the early stages all the qualities will be almost the same. Later, there may be some difference. He held that there would be at least co-education of boys and girls till the age of fourteen. Artificial segregation of boys and girls will not lead to their development, but either to perversion or to an extremely one-sided education.

If anyone can reform society, it is the teacher, not the police or the military. A teacher is a bridge between the past and the future. He has to bring about a peaceful social transformation. The teacher's duty is to understand all trends of thought, to transform men's minds and hearts, and to point the way to a transformation of their lives.

A teacher needs to possess at least three qualities. The first is that he must be an affectionate and living friend to his students. This is of such importance that without it he can never be a teacher at all. The second is that he himself must be a tireless seeker after knowledge, always studying, continually adding new items to his store. He must become an ocean of learning, a votary of science. The teacher needs a third quality also. Political activity has a powerful attraction for students today, and the students are under the care of teachers. Teachers are in a position of great authority and they should keep clear of all political involvement. If a teacher gets involved in politics, he is no longer his own master; he is a mere tool in the hands of another and loses his independence.

Regarding the duties of the students, Vinoba said, "The first duty of students is to preserve the full independence of their minds. If anyone has a right to full freedom, it is the student. Knowledge cannot be had without faith, but it is equally essential that along with faith he should have intellectual freedom. The second duty of students is to exercise self-control. Only a man who can control himself has the right to freedom. A student must feel confident that he can carry out his own resolutions. The third duty of students is to devote themselves to service. Knowledge cannot be had without service. The leaders have experience, and they open their hearts to those who serve them, and give them all they have. Students then must devote themselves to the service of elders and parents, of the poor and the afflicted, and of society. They should not think that this service will leave them no time for study; they should have faith that knowledge is acquired by service. The fourth duty of students is to be alert to what is going on around them. They should study all the movements of the modern world and the current ideologies with open minds. Their outlook must be broad and they must not allow themselves to think within narrow limits".[4]

The biggest reform that we will have to be done in the educational system is to re-establish the former relationship between the teacher and the pupil.

REFERENCES

1. *Harijan*, 19-12-38.
2. *Ibid.*, 2-3-47.
3. *Ibid.*, 10-7-54.
4. Vinoba, *Thoughts on Education*, pp. 185-190.

BIBLIOGRAPHY

On Gandhi

Arunachalam, K., *Khadi Economics: A Few Aspects*, Koodal Publishers, Madurai, 1974.

Bharathi, K.S., *Foundations of Gandhian Thought*, Dattsons Publishers, Nagpur, 1987.

Bharathi, K.S., *Socio-religious Thought of Mahatma Gandhi*, Dattsons Publishers, Nagpur, 1989.

Bharathi, K.S., *Gandhi and Humanity*, Gandhi Seva Ashram Samiti, Nagpur, 1988.

Bharathi, K.S., *The Philosophy of Sarvodya*, Indus Publishing Company, New Delhi, 1990.

Bharathi, K.S. *Satyagraha of Mahatma Gandhi*, Indus Publishing Company, New Delhi, 1990.

Bharathi, K.S., *Gandhi and Nehru*, Indus Publishing Company, New Delhi, 1990.

Bose, N.K., *Selections from Gandhi*, Navajeevan Publishing House, Ahmedabad, 1950.

Dhawan, G.N., *Political Philosophy of Mahatma Gandhi*, Navajeevan Publishing House, Ahmedabad, 1946.

Ganguli, B.N., *Gandhi's Social Philosophy: Perspective and Relevance*, Vikas Publishing House, Delhi, 1973.

Gandhi, M.K., *An Autobiography*, Navajeevan Publishing House, Ahmedabad, 1957.

Gandhi, M.K., *Basic Education*, Navajeevan Publishing House, Ahmedabad, 1951.

Gandhi, M.K., *Hind Swaraj*, Navajeevan Publishing House, Ahmedabad, 1938.

Gandhi, M.K., *Hindu Dharma*, Navajeevan Publishing House, Ahmedabad, 1950.

Homer, A.J., *Religion for Peace*, Bharatiya Vidya Bhavan, Bombay, 1973.

Kripalani, J.B., *Gandhian Thought*, Gandhi Smarak Nidhi, New Delhi, 1961.

Kumarappa, J.C., *Gandhian Thought*, Vora & Co., Bombay, 1951.

Mashruwala, K.G., *Towards Sarvodaya Order*, Navajeevan Publishing House, Ahmedabad, 1971.

Mehta, J.K., *Gandhian Thought*, Asian Publishing House, New Delhi, 1985.

Nanda, B.R., *Gandhi and His Critics*, Oxford University Press, Delhi, 1985.

Patil, S.H., *Gandhi and Swaraj*, Deep and Deep Publications, New Delhi, 1983.

Radhakrishnan, S., *Mahatma Gandhi - 100 Years*, Orient Longmans, Delhi, 1968.

Ramachandran, G., *The Economics of Peace*, ABSS Sangh, Wardha, 1952.

Ramachandran, G., and Mahadevan, T.K. (Eds.), *Gandhi, His Relevance for Our Times*, Bharatiya Vidya Bhavan, Bombay, 1972.

Ramjee Singh, *The Relevance of Gandhian Thought*, Classical Publishing Company, New Delhi, 1982.

Romain, Rolland, *Mahatma Gandhi*, Allen and Unwin, London, 1924.

Sethi, J.D., *Gandhi Today*, Vikas Publishing House, Delhi, 1978.

Sukhla, C.S., *Gandhi's View of Life*, Bharatiya Vidya Bhavan, Bombay, 1960.

Varma, V.P., *The Political Philosophy of Mahatma Gandhi and Sarvodaya*, Lakshmi Narain Agarwal, Agra, 1959.

Viswanath, T., *The Social and Political Philosophy of Sarvodaya After Gandhi*, Sarva Seva Sangh Prakashan, Varanasi 1965.

On Vinoba

Bhave, Vinoba, *Talks on the Gita*, Sarva Seva Sangh, Varanasi

Bhave, Vinoba, *The Essence of the Quran*, Sarva Seva Sangh, Varanasi.

Bhave, Vinoba, *Thoughts on Education*, Sarva Seva Sangh, Varanasi.

Bhave, Vinoba, *Democratic Values*, Sarva Seva Sangh, Varanasi.

Bhave, Vinoba, *Swarajya Sastra*, Sarva Seva Sangh, Varanasi.

Bhave, Vinoba, *Shanti Sena*, Sarva Seva Sangh, Varanasi.

Bhave, Vinoba, *Language Problem*, Sarva Seva Sangh, Varanasi.

Bhave, Vinoba, *Bhoodan Yajna*, Navjeevan Publishing House, Ahmedabad.

Bhave, Vinoba, *Gram Swaraj: Our Birthright*, Sarvodaya Prachuralaya, Tanjore.

Desai, N., *Shanti Sena in India*, Sarva Seva Sangh, Varanasi.

Groom, D., *With Vinoba*, Sarva Seva Sangh, Varanasi.

Jaju, S., *The Philosophy of Sampattidan*, Sarvodaya Prachuralaya, Tanjore.

Kriplani, J.B., *Sarvodaya and Democracy*, Sarvodaya Prachuralaya, Tanjore.

Misra, B.R., *V. for Vinoba — The Economics of the Bhoodan Movement*, Orient Longmans, Delhi.

Narayan, S., *One Week with Vinoba*, A.I.C.C., New Delhi.
Narayan, J., *From Socialism to Sarvodaya*, Sarva Seva Sangh, Varanasi.
Nargolkar, V., *The Creed of Saint Vinoba*, Bharatiya Vidya Bhavan, Bombay.
Ram, S., *Vinoba and His Mission*, Sarva Seva Sangh, Varanasi.
Shah, K., *Vinoba Life and Mission*, Sarva Seva Sangh, Varanasi.
Sharma, J.S., *Vinoba and Bhoodan*, Bibliography, Indian National Congress, New Delhi.
Tandon, P.D., *Vinoba Bhave: The Man and His Mission*, Vora and Co., Bombay.
Tandon, V., *Sarvodaya after Gandhi*, Sarva Seva Sangh, Varanasi.
Tandon, V., *Selections from Vinoba*, Sarva Seva Sangh, Varanasi.

Magazines and Journals

Bhoodan
Bhoodan Yajna
Gandhi Marg
Gogras
Harijan
Khadi Jagat
Khadi World
Maitri
Sarvodaya
Young India

INDEX